Sheconomics

Sheconomics

Add power
to your purse
with the ultimate
money makeover

Karen Pine and
Simonne Gnessen

headline

First published in 2009
by HEADLINE PUBLISHING GROUP

1

Cataloguing in Publication Data is available from the British Library

Paperback ISBN 978 0 7553 1827 8

Typeset in Helvetica Neue by Ellipsis Books Limited, Glasgow

Printed and bound in Great Britain by
Clays Ltd, St Ives plc

Headline's policy is to use papers that are natural, renewable
and recyclable products and made from wood grown in sustainable forests.
The logging and manufacturing processes are expected to conform
to the environmental regulations of the country of origin.

HEADLINE PUBLISHING GROUP
An Hachette Livre UK Company
338 Euston Road
London NW1 3BH

www.headline.co.uk
www.hachettelivre.co.uk
www.sheconomics.co.uk

Contents

Preface   1

Chapter 1   **Welcome to Sheconomics**   3

Chapter 2   **Law 1: Take emotional control**   8

Chapter 3   **Law 2: Go beyond beliefs**   33

Chapter 4   **Law 3: Spend with power**   63

Chapter 5   **Law 4: Have goals**   121

Chapter 6   **Law 5: Look debt in the face**   156

Chapter 7   **Law 6: Share Financial Intimacies**   215

Chapter 8   **Law 7: Know tomorrow comes**   261

Chapter 9   **A day in the life of ... A top Sheconomist**   321

Index   339

For Ben and Emma

We'd like to convey our heartfelt thanks to everyone who helped us get our passion for Sheconomics onto the printed page. To all the women who shared their money stories with us, and Simonne's clients whose case studies bring this book alive with personal experiences, thank you. We couldn't have done it without you. To our wonderful agent, Sheila Crowley, for making it happen in the first place and then being a consistent, ever-smiling source of support, knowledge and encouragement. To the brilliant foreign rights teams for spreading the Sheconomics message across the globe. To our editor Carly Cook for feeling as passionate about Sheconomics as we do and whose amazing professionalism, insight and positive energy have made the book the great read that it is. To Josh Ireland, Helena Towers, Ruth Jeffery and the rest of the top-rate team at Headline for all their hard work and dedication. To Rona Johnson for copy-editing extraordinaire. To those involved in the research, the inspirational Jessica Chivers, and to Avie Nash for handling all the survey data. Finally, to our partners, families and friends for their tolerance, love and support – thank you.

PREFACE

'Money? It's for spending isn't it? I love to shop. I shop when I'm bored, stressed or when someone's upset me. I splashed out on a Whistles dress the other day but now I've gone off it. Sometimes I hate myself, especially when I look at my scary credit card debt. I need to get control of my money and start saving. I need to understand my feelings about money. And right now I need . . . I need those gorgeous pink peep-toe stilettos I spotted yesterday.'

This quote sums up the complicated relationship a lot of women have with money. A struggle that many men don't have and will never understand.

That's why this is a book for women everywhere. We've talked to hundreds of women about money. From women on City bonuses to women on benefits. They have confided their deepest money secrets to us and we're hugely grateful to them for their complete honesty. Most of the women came to us to sort out their relationship with money – that's why we've called them trainee Sheconomists. We've designed our seven Laws of Sheconomics with them – and you – in mind.

We've tried not to load the book up with numbers. But where figures are quoted they are for illustrative purposes only. We know things like interest rates change more often than the fashion for skinny jeans, so don't take them too literally. What's more important is our message, which we believe holds up, no matter what the FTSE is doing.

This book will show you that money doesn't have to be a tricky mystery. It is all about confidence. If you do find any 'foreign' financial lingo here, just flick to 'The slightly confused girl's guide to the world of finance' glossary at the back. Always seek independent financial advice if you're uncertain.

We hope you will love reading this book as much as we've loved writing it. But more than anything, we hope that you will find it useful. There are some Do Something Different exercises that we hope will help you incorporate our advice into your everyday lives. Some of them might seem a bit leftfield, but they're actually based on sound psychological theory, FIT Science, developed by Professor Ben Fletcher. We're thrilled with this new field of Sheconomics and incredibly excited about the new, sassy band of Sheconomists that it will unleash on the land. Go forth and multiply (your money that is!).

Karen and Simonne

Chapter 1
Welcome to Sheconomics

How we feel about money is crucial to how we manage it. Now, more than ever, women need to take control of their financial destiny. This book brings you the tools necessary to explore your complicated relationship with money – we also hope you'll have some fun along the way. We believe you will emerge from reading this book brimming with the fiscal know-how to put yourself on a much firmer financial footing. You will take control of your money, instead of your money controlling you.

Money management might not be top of your list of wildly exciting things to do but, once you understand money, you'll discover the thrill of earning it, managing it, not worrying about it, as well as spending it.

Naturally, we hope you're prepared to do some soul-searching along the way, because understanding what makes us tick in relation to money is a big part of becoming a top Sheconomist.

Forget all the economic wizardry and the dull number-crunching so loved by the financial press. Where's the stuff that women want to know? There's not even a passing nod to all the tensions, pressures and moments of angst that occupy a woman's money world: how scary all the paperwork can be when you haven't got a clue what it means; how to deal with a shopping hangover when you've gone into debt for a coat that no longer fits; how to persuade a reluctant boyfriend to go anywhere near a mortgage broker; how to reach even the vaguest idea of how much you'll need to live on when you retire.

We have met hundreds of women who've confided their financial secrets to us. All of them were incredibly competent in other areas of life but, somehow, along the way they forgot to plan for the future.

Our survey of 700 women also told us that:
- 75 per cent shop to cheer themselves up
- 79 per cent wish they had more self-control when it comes to spending
- more than 50 per cent overspend to impress others
- 70 per cent had worried about money in the last seven days

The way in which women deal with money depends on so many different factors but we know – because we're women, too – that it's driven largely by emotions. We also know that our emotions can be one of the biggest obstacles to financial success and we're going to address that, not in a dry, bank-managery kind of way; more in a let's-talk-about-it-over-a-glass-of-wine kind of way.

Why do women use shopping as a pick-me-up? Is the female of the species really more debt-prone than the male? Why can we hold our own in the boardroom yet go to pieces in the changing room? Why do we blithely stick our fingers in our ears at the mention of investments, ISAs and interest rates? We plan holidays and weddings with military precision. Why not pensions? We can talk with confidence and sensitivity about personal problems, why not money worries?

It's not that women are worse than men with money, it's just that we're different. As with many other aspects of our lives, when it comes to money matters we're more susceptible to being affected by and reacting on the basis of our emotions. Sheconomics is about connecting with those money emotions.

The more women have been sharing their financial experiences with us, the wider we have found the gulf between the sexes to be. For example, it's hard to imagine a man saying:

'When I feel negative about my appearance I think buying new clothes/shoes will make me feel better about myself, but often it leads to me becoming more upset.'

'I only shop for shoes when I'm overweight. I have more than one hundred and fifty pairs of shoes so I must feel overweight quite a lot!'

'Since I moved in with my partner we've been going through a rocky patch and my shopping is getting out of control.'

'I know I'm not earning anywhere near what I'm worth but I'm sure they won't give me a pay rise.'

We know that lots of women are fixated on money. They may even be suffering from what we call Money Anxiety Disorder (MAD). That's not good. Women worry more than men do about every aspect of owing money, from mortgage repayments to taking out a loan to buy a car, to anxiety about the cost of living in general – 75 per cent of the women we surveyed said it worries them, whereas other surveys have shown that only 50 per cent of men in the same situation were concerned. So it's no surprise that women tend to bear the brunt of financial pressure in families.

As a Sheconomist you won't depend on men for your financial security, nor will you rely on men to make your financial decisions for you. Forget about being taken care of by a handsome prince with a portfolio to die for. Independence is a far more attractive option.

Your relationship with money is out of control? You've been putting off things you shouldn't? Read on. This is about making a new life choice. We're here to help uncover what's been getting in the way, work through issues and break through obstacles so that you can move forward. Our 7 Laws of Sheconomics sum up everything women need to take and remain in full financial control. We hope they will simplify the world of money for you, making the future stress-free and brighter.

The 7 Laws of Sheconomics

Law 1: Take emotional control
Be aware of how your emotions affect the way you behave with money

Law 2: Go beyond beliefs
Know that your financial beliefs can become reality

Law 3: Spend with power
Make sure all your spending decisions are made for the right reasons

Law 4: Have goals
Make your money fit your life plan

Law 5: Look debt in the face
Face up to what you owe and decide how to pay it back

Law 6: Share financial intimacies
Talk openly and honestly about money

Law 7: Know tomorrow comes
Take action now for a secure future

Chapter 2
Law 1: Take emotional control

> Drained of emotion, money is nothing. It has no power except the power we give it. And what we give it determines what it gives back to us.
>
> Grainne O'Malley

Around 3.8 million people in the UK say money worries have kept them off work, a staggering 10.8 million blame money for their relationship problems and almost 20 per cent of people from either sex with money concerns complain of a loss of libido.

As we said in Chapter 1, women's attitude to money is shaped by emotion. Strong emotional responses can hit when we least expect them and hijack rational behaviour, as these trainee Sheconomists found:

'My partner asked me an innocent money question the other day and I flew off the handle.'

'My best mate recently got a massive pay rise and company car allowance and although I was happy for her I felt eaten up by jealousy, too.'

'I panic every time I hear the words "credit crunch".'

'My pay rise is overdue but I'm too embarrassed to remind my boss.'

Thus, financial decisions aren't always rooted in common sense. When you face a crisis, a tug-of-war goes on between opposing pathways within the brain and the more you let your emotions win over, the more trouble you'll have applying logic and reason. One trainee noticed how irrational she can be:

'I've been struck by how money has a different value attached to it depending on what I'm buying. I easily spend fifty pounds on dinner and don't bat an eyelid. But if I bought a jumper for that I'd worry that I was splashing my money around. Strange really!'

The same amount of money, £50 in the case above, should have the same significance under all circumstances – but we know it doesn't. Psychologists call this 'mental accounting': we justify the expense of a designer outfit for a job interview by convincing ourselves the extra earnings will cover it, we spend £100 on a face cream but tell ourselves it's OK because the money came from a tax rebate.

In one of our surveys asking women about their emotional spending, more than 50 per cent said they go shopping when they feel low. One of our trainees told us:

'I buy very expensive items when I'm emotional – normally after a relationship break-up. And I'm not talking small stuff here; I bought a car and a house when I felt like this. The house, I hasten to add, was a disastrous decision.'

But emotions aren't always easy to identify, as another trainee Sheconomist told us:

'I cannot manage my money whatsoever. I place the blame on my partner but I believe there's more to it than that. I just don't know what!'

Taking emotional control is all about being able to replace the emotions that interfere and hold you back with emotions that motivate and move you forward.

Some of the Do Something Different (DSD) exercises in this chapter – and others throughout the book – will help you to identify the triggers that can spin you into a positive, emotional high or plunge you into money misery. Such money-misery triggers may be a relationship problem, a food issue, boredom or fear of responsibility.

Whatever, you're not wedded to those negative reactions and can shed them by doing something different.

For most people, money is more than just notes and coins. It signifies power, status, comfort, confidence, happiness – indeed, a whole array of emotionally loaded stuff. As women we play out our deepest fears and desires in the way we behave with money, yet talking about money is virtually taboo. We overstate the 'privacy' of money to such an extent that, sometimes, we even find it tricky to face the reality of our own financial situation ourselves. For example, 25 per cent of people in the UK *never* look at their credit card statements.

As a first step to becoming a top Sheconomist, this chapter talks through some typical, difficult money emotions, helps you work out what yours are and shows how to stop them coming between you and the right money decisions. You'll discover how to strip money of its emotional significance thereby setting you free to take your finances in hand.

MONEY MADNESS

Psychologists are rather fond of getting people to play something called the Ultimatum Game and it is actually quite revealing. It shows that we make monetary decisions using more than a mental calculator – a whole gamut of emotions come into play, too. It goes like this:

Imagine you and a complete stranger have to split £10 between you. She's been given the £10 and told to share it with you – in *any* way she likes. She can decide how much to keep and how much to give to you. There's just one condition: if you refuse what you are offered, neither of you get anything.

What would you turn down? How about if she gave you £1 and kept £9 herself? Would you refuse it, to punish her selfishness?

There's only one rational thing to do. Accept anything she offers. After all, it's money for nothing. An offer of £1 is £1 more than you had before you started. But in experiments most people (in the original experiment the figure was as high as 80 per cent, though a more recent study found this rate to be nearer 50 per cent) turned down anything below £2.50 and so got nothing. The emotional part of the brain sabotaged the rational part. Instead of making a level-headed decision for their own financial advancement, they opted for the short-term emotional satisfaction of getting back at the stranger for being unfair.

In one University of Cambridge study, players with low levels of a brain chemical called serotonin fared worst. Serotonin levels are boosted by diet so they suggest tucking into a chicken sandwich before negotiating a pay deal!

DO SOMETHING DIFFERENT: WORK OUT THE REAL COST TO YOU

Calculate roughly how much you earn an hour. Take the cost of one of those 'must-haves' and convert it into the number of hours you would have to work to pay for it. This way, you strip money of its emotional significance and view it in a more functional way.

Feelings about money

Here are just a few of the niggling, troublesome sentiments that women tell us bother them when it comes to money. Do you recognize any of them?

- I'm ashamed to own up to not understanding my finances
- I'm totally confused when it comes to making any money decision
- I don't feel grown up when it comes to money
- Money worries keep me awake at night
- I'm scared to face up to the amount of debt I'm in
- I'm angry at myself for how much money I've wasted over the years
- Shopping is a great way to lift my spirits when I'm feeling low

If you recognise three or more of these statements then you'll know that money and emotions are often inseparable.

But we are all different and we each have a different emotional relationship with money: one woman's fear might be another woman's assurance. You must have friends, for example, who seem to sail through life barely giving their bank statements a second glance, even if they're always in the red. Meanwhile, the rest of us obsess about what we earn or owe.

The fact is the emotions you feel about money have nothing to do with how much of it you've got. Regardless of how high your salary is, if you are up against a huge block of negative money emotions, you are going to feel financially fragile. Or even phobic. Or out of control.

Emotional management is where financial management begins. So, let's look at your money emotions and how we can deal with them.

What are your money emotions?

Here's an emotion-recognition exercise to help you give a name to those funny feelings that creep up whenever you have to deal with money.

First, read through the groups (lists) of words in the table below then mull over your own feelings about money matters in general. Next, circle any words in the table that strike a chord with how you feel. Don't spend too much time on it – just follow your gut instinct.

Anger	Fear	Enjoyment	Disgust	Shame
Fury	Denial	Happiness	Contempt	Guilt
Jealousy	Dread	Relief	Scorn	Embarrassment
Resentment	Anxiety	Contentment	Indignation	Remorse
Irritability	Apprehension	Pride	Disrespect	Humiliation
Hostility	Terror	Thrill	Revulsion	Awkwardness
Rage	Edginess	Gratification	Abhorrence	Regret
Annoyance	Panic	Satisfaction	Aversion	Contrition

There are so many words for emotions we couldn't even begin to include them all here. But psychologists have come up with a handful of core emotions which may mix and merge into an infinite range of moods and feelings, much as the primary colours – red, blue and yellow – may blend into myriad shades. Take a look at where most of your circled words appear and you'll probably find them clustered around one or two groups. The group heading (Anger, Fear, etc.) describes the core emotion at the root of your feelings.

Here, we explore four of the troublesome core money emotions – fear, anger, disgust and shame – alongside a selection of DSD exercises designed to help you manage your emotions.

Fear

Fear is the big bad wolf of money emotions and it comes in different guises.

'I'm too frightened to even look at my bank statements because I know I won't like what I see. My debts are growing, but I don't know how to get them under control. Even if I did have enough money to start investing in sensible things I'd be terrified of making the wrong decision and losing my money.'

Being in debt, or knowing your finances are spiralling out of control are both common causes of deeply fearful money emotions – the kind that bring you out in a cold sweat at two o'clock in the morning. In the face of real fear caused by a real money problem many women feel powerless, and may be so paralysed by worry that they can't even bring themselves to open their credit card statement, let alone start dealing with the problem.

DO SOMETHING DIFFERENT: DARE TO GO THERE

Buy a weekend newspaper and browse the money section. You might be pleasantly surprised at what you can pick up from other people's experiences in the real life money stories.

Even when you are solvent, fear can strike. Perhaps you are so terrified of making the wrong investment decision that you allow somebody else in your life – parent, partner, trusted friend – to make it for you; worse still, you may simply do nothing at all with your money. Fear may blinker you, so that you stick with safe, familiar financial products even if there are more profitable alternatives with little extra risk. Are you frightened into waiting so long for the perfect moment to make that financial move only to realize, time and again, that the moment has been and gone? Think, for example, of all the people who jumped too late onto the buy-to-let bandwagon and found that their mortgage had gone up and the bottom had dropped out of the housing market.

DO SOMETHING DIFFERENT: GET ORGANIZED

A huge, untidy pile of paperwork is scary and unhelpful. An orderly set of clearly labelled files – in bright colours if you like – is much less daunting. The very act of filing your bills and statements will begin to put you back in control.

Fear of running out of money one day can lead to an almost miserly mentality which, in turn, can result in adopting an austere way of life coupled with the inability to enjoy. For example:

'I am dreadfully anxious about money. I'm hopeless at spending any on myself, rarely go shopping and frequently worry about being broke.'

In contrast, this form of fear can, as this trainee Sheconomist told us, lead to unnecessary spending and hoarding on a large scale:

'My husband is out of work but I can't seem to stop myself buying – clothes, shoes, things for the children and stuff we'll need over the next few months. I buy large quantities of everything as a sort of insurance policy. So the kids have three coats and four pairs of shoes each – more than they need – and I worry that the things we need won't be in the shops by the time I have the money. Winter is coming and I think, yes, we do need these waterproofs, even though we can't afford them.'

DO SOMETHING DIFFERENT: FIND A MONEY BUDDY

If you feel you can't keep your bulk-buying in check, take a sensible friend along on your shopping trip. With someone there to shine a spotlight on your multiple madnesses you're less likely to go over the top!

Do you ever feel anxious when you come across someone who's doing better than you? Psychologists call this fear of being left out reference anxiety. It's when we use someone else's level of success to gauge our own.

DO SOMETHING DIFFERENT: CHOOSE A DIFFERENT COMPARATOR

If you're eaten up with reference anxiety, perhaps you're comparing yourself with others too much.

Stop reading magazines that make you feel you don't measure up. Write out a list of the things that mean success to *you* and gauge yourself only against that. And don't forget that having good friends, a healthy lifestyle and a fulfilling job are great achievements.

I (Karen) know a great couple who love the Mediterranean way of life and have a second home in Tuscany. So I invited them to dinner with another couple, who also have a second home in Tuscany. Except the second couple have a bigger property than the first. With a vineyard. Did their common love of Tuscany unite these four as friends? No, it did not. Reference anxiety hit couple number one so badly that all four ended up arguing: who'd been going there longest, who knew most locals. The washing up had never looked so appealing as it did that evening. By the time they were competing over how many local festivals they'd personally organized for the villagers I was cleaning behind the oven.

Anger

Anger over money can be the result of our own actions or a response to what others have done. It can have a variety of different causes from jealousy to resentment at being unfairly treated. Everyone gets angry from time to time – it's a normal emotion – but it becomes unhealthy if you turn to money to help resolve your rage. When we take our anger shopping it can unleash a credit card-spending disaster, as this trainee Sheconomist found:

'I'm having a tough time because I've just been let down again by my boyfriend and I am furious with him. So I've been buying treats for myself because I think I deserve them: new sunglasses, a bag and an Armani suit. The last time this happened I went on a shopping spree and bought everything I liked, without even looking at the price tags. It was kind of cathartic at the time but in the end I had to resolve my debts with an IVA (Individual Voluntary Arrangement).'

DO SOMETHING DIFFERENT: TAKE THE HEAT OUT

Don't have overheated discussions about money. Do something else with the energy you're experiencing: go for a walk or take a few deep breaths to calm yourself before going back to the topic.

When you are feeling overwrought, hormonal, stressed or have just had an argument these are the times NOT to hit the shops.

Disgust

While it's wrong to worship money and make it your be-all

and end-all, contempt for it can be dysfunctional. For some, like this trainee Sheconomist, disgust can manifest as a strong physical and emotional aversion to money:

'Discussing money makes me feel ill – like a child who's been caught doing something they shouldn't have. And I actually hate shopping with a passion.'

DO SOMETHING DIFFERENT: PUSH YOUR BOUNDARIES

If you are over-cautious with money, experiment by telling yourself you _can_ afford something, then buy it and see how you feel. You can always take it back!

Or if you feel contempt for money, go to a posh hotel that feels out of your league. Just order a coffee and enjoy the experience.

Disgust may stem from a lack of trust in others, or a dislike of those who have money. What's striking about this is that, apart from not enjoying the good side of money, you may be unconsciously pushing it from your life. You may even sabotage your own financial success. One of our trainee Sheconomists felt strongly that her anti-money emotions became reality:

'I think somehow that I attract more bills when I hate money and yet when I relax about it and allow myself to like it more, it seems to flow more naturally and I have more'

Shame

Everyone's discussing ISAs. You are too embarrassed to admit that you don't even know what an ISA is. You're red faced and feeling twitchy. Many women tell us they feel ashamed and inadequate because of their financial illiteracy.

DO SOMETHING DIFFERENT: WISE UP

Take a look around the Financial Services Authority's website www.moneymadeclear.fsa.gov.uk

It cuts out jargon and simplifies money matters.

Maybe everyone in your family clammed up when money was mentioned? Then it would hardly come as a huge shock if we said this is why you still treat it as a taboo subject, as was the case with this trainee Sheconomist:

'Money has always been unmentionable in any relationship I've had. It was the same way with my family. Even now if ever the subject gets raised, a volcano of emotion erupts!'

Do you shy away from asking for money? Can't bear the cringing discomfort money-talk evokes? This is why many women (but, interestingly, fewer men) shrink from asking for a pay rise – they're embarrassed about appearing pushy. It's also why women are less likely to haggle over the price of a car, negotiate the best mobile phone deal or ask a lender for a payment break.

DO SOMETHING DIFFERENT: ASK FOR MONEY

Chase up debts. Know what you're worth and don't be afraid to ask for what is due to you. Renegotiate your hourly rate and/or tell your manager when you know you are due for a rise (a Wednesday afternoon is said to be the best time). Remember, if you don't ask you don't get.

The growth of the internet has opened up a whole new arena for exploiting the 'secret shame of shopping' and women represent 60 per cent of the online shopping market. Hanging out in shops is conspicuous and public; internet buying is covert, private, even clandestine – it's easy to hide what you're doing. After all, it doesn't look like shopping. In fact, it looks reassuringly like work – I'm writing this book but I have several net-a-porter pages open behind my word document. And the fact that I know my credit card number off by heart is a sure sign I've been typing it in too frequently.

The secrecy element, however, reinforces the perception that spending money is bad or naughty. The ensuing shame for an online shopping addict means the fun is short lived. One of our trainee Sheconomists told us how she finds the whole buying online experience naughty-but-nice:

'When I'm low or bored I browse eBay looking for things to buy. I spend a lot on the internet as it feels secretive and naughty and self-indulgent and no one has to know about it.'

But that secrecy can be dangerous. It keeps your bad habit buried and stops you dealing with your shame.

Early money messages

'I live alone and often won't even tell my friends what I've bought because I feel so guilty or afraid they'll judge my spending habits. When I was a child, my mother would shop in secret from my father and then tell me not to wear the new stuff for a while so I could honestly say I'd had it for ages, so I know it goes way back.'

Children tend to be strongly influenced by their parents' attitudes and behaviour. You might remember as a child witnessing your parents' whispered conversations, rows or icy silences and being left in no doubt that something unpleasant was going on.

In homes where one parent spends recklessly, perhaps because of blatant irresponsibility, or a gambling or alcohol addiction, the whole family is affected. Children growing up in an environment such as this may develop deep and long-lasting feelings of insecurity about money.

> **Juanita's story**
>
> Juanita grew up with an alcoholic father and is now a psychotherapist. She believes that children who are raised by an unpredictable parent live with the constant fear that they could suddenly lose everything.
>
> 'In later years,' says Juanita, 'no matter how much money you have, that fear of being broke doesn't leave you. It's always there in the background, the way it was when you were a kid – living hand-to-mouth and never knowing whether your dad's drinking binge meant there was no money for food.'

Money may also be lavished on others in the hope of salving a guilty conscience. One of our trainee Sheconomists describes how she came to be saddled with such a legacy:

'I have a problem with compulsive spending. I "spoil" myself constantly, whether it's simply a bottle of wine or a pair of boots, I have to buy myself something every day. I was given handouts as a child to salve my parents'

consciences about divorcing and I don't think I ever really learned the importance of money.'

The answer is to deal with such emotions, not spend them.

Where do your money emotions come from?

Mary's story

It was clear from the start that Mary was painstakingly cautious about money. She arrived at our first meeting with a metal box containing all her finance-related papers. She was meticulous about her filing, and super-organized when it came to money. But Mary's efficiency was hiding a whole raft of financial fears.

We'd talked for only a few minutes when Mary told me a story about her father: 'My dad was promised a good pension but by the time he'd retired rising inflation had rendered it practically worthless. All those years of pension payments, for nothing.'

However much I explained that her pensions were linked to inflation, Mary dreaded that she, too, might end up penniless. This belief was played out in Mary's money behaviour. In addition to her pensions, she had squirreled away hundreds of thousands of pounds in savings and investments, yet she remained convinced there would never be enough.

In reality, Mary had plenty put away for the future. Living in fear was crazy. The constant stress she was feeling about her financial security was sapping her enjoyment of life.

We looked at all the evidence – savings accounts and investments all well-selected and balanced to avoid risk plus the healthy projections for her pensions. And I was able to show Mary, in a host of different ways, how financially secure she was, that there was no evidence to support her belief that she'd be hard-up in retirement – unlike her father.

This was the point at which Mary truly began to believe that she was safe. Almost immediately her outlook began to change – lighten up – and she is finally able to enjoy life more.

Troll as far back as you can through your own money memories. Do they connect with your current attitudes to money?

Talking through your responses to the questions below with someone who has known you well throughout your life should help to clarify your relationship with money.

- Did you feel rich or poor as you were growing up?
- How did that compare to other people you knew?
- What role did money play in your childhood?
- What happy memories do you recall about money?
- What unhappy memories do you recall about money?
- How did it feel when you earned money for the first time?
- How do you think any of this impacts on you now?
- What are your biggest fears or concerns about money?

Learn anything from this exercise? It's amazing how we all experience different emotions when it comes to money and how much they shape whatever strategy we employ to deal with our money.

Bargain-hunting, gain or shame

I (Simonne) put my bargain-hunting tendencies down to something I experienced at the age of eleven. It was 1977, the year of the Queen's Silver Jubilee, and a travel agent was offering two-week holidays in the Algarve at 1952 prices – a holiday that my family could never have afforded to pay full price for. There was only limited availability on the offer so for two days we took turns queuing and we were in luck. We had an incredible, unforgettable holiday.

Ever since then I've connected putting effort into getting a good deal with huge fun and excitement. My experience has, in fact, inspired a helpful money-saving habit – to ensure the best deal, I always compare prices online before I buy. There's just one caveat: I have to be on guard not to buy something just because it's a bargain – which, I admit, I have been known to do.

For me (Karen) an early bargain had less positive connotations. My parents were not well off but I went to a posh school that topped up the fee income by flogging expensive sports equipment. At the start of one term our parents were 'invited' to buy one of two hockey sticks for us. One was shiny navy and silver and ludicrously overpriced, the other – brown, dull and lacklustre – was half-price on a special offer.

My dad knew I worked hard to avoid hockey so he insisted I have the cheap one – a perfectly rational decision. But I was the only girl in my class with that stick (I *know* all twelve year-olds say this sort of thing but I'm sure it was true). Everyone knew mine was the bargain buy and, to me, it screamed 'cheapskate'. Ever since, I've linked bargains with feelings of shame: for years I wouldn't be seen dead in a Pound Saver or charity shop in case someone saw me.

Now, I've learned to admire people who won't pay over the odds for anything but I still, sometimes, feel the old shame in the background and I am still slightly embarrassed at taking a 'reduced' item to the checkout.

So, I don't really share the thrill of a good deal that Simonne describes and that means I probably miss out on some good bargains.

DO SOMETHING DIFFERENT: CONFRONT YOUR MONEY STRATEGY

Explore your money strategy: work out what it is and where it comes from.

Are you a spender or a saver? Do you plan for the future or spend tomorrow's money today?

Talk to someone who knew you well throughout your childhood and adolescence – a family member or long-standing family friend. Discuss with them what money messages you grew up with and consider the impact they are having on the decisions you're making about money now. Take time to answer and discuss the 'Where do your money emotions come from?' questions.

Money personalities

Many psychologists have entertained notions of money personalities and much has been written about people's different money profiles. But, while it is great fun to read and speculate whether you're a 'safety player', a 'hunter', a 'producer' or, perhaps, a 'high roller', do avoid labelling yourself as any particular money personality.

A label can become an excuse to persist with an inappropriate behaviour pattern – a means of avoiding taking responsibility for your actions. For example, the safety player may take comfort in being labelled *naturally* risk averse but there is an important distinction between playing safe, taking calculated risks and moving forward and being too scared to do anything and going financially nowhere. We want you to be free-thinking, responsible and flexibly minded and that means no labels and NOT having a money personality.

Emotional reconditioning
Here are our top tips for not being at the mercy of your money emotions:

1. Spot the emotion Be as specific as you can and instead of acting when in an emotional state, stop and think for a minute about how it is you're feeling.

2. Identify the trigger Is it a reaction to something real that you're facing now, or has it been sparked off by an old memory or previous experience?

3. Challenge the emotion Is it useful in your current financial situation? If it is warning you of real danger, heed it. If it's a gut feeling that you can trust, go with it. But if it's reinforcing bad habits, feel free to ditch it.

4. Connect with your goal Shift your thoughts onto whatever you are aiming for, not your feelings. That'll help motivate you towards taking action to change things.

5. Break free Do Something Different (we give you plenty of ideas) to change the emotion or act despite it.

My Sheconomics Checklist
Law 1

Are you taking emotional control? ✓

I am aware of my emotions about money	
I've put my past behind me when it comes to money emotions	
I can treat money neutrally and make rational, unemotional decisions about it	
I'm not afraid to Do Something Different with money	
I don't label myself with a money personality	

Chapter 3
Law 2: Go beyond beliefs

'I have not failed. I've just found 10,000 ways that won't work.'

Thomas Edison (inventor).

Our beliefs influence the way we behave and, in turn, what we do or do not achieve. If, for example, you believe that you're bad with money, you probably will be. On the other hand, if you believe that riches will be yours, then more than likely you will, indeed, be rich.

For better or worse, our monetary beliefs can be extraordinary powerful. But beware, misplaced conviction can distort financial reality and drive us to dangerous extremes – an addiction to gambling, for example, when regardless of risk or consequence the belief that the next bet will be a winner drives the gambler on.

Several years ago I (Simonne) underwent a bit of a transformation. I moved from being a traditional financial advisor to become a financial coach and, with that, I started having very different conversations with the people who came through my door. The tired old financial services industry questions took a back seat. It soon became obvious to me that most women's financial problems were either the result of or complicated by their underlying attitude to money alongside a variety of personal issues and/or self-limiting beliefs.

When women were struggling with money problems the questions that really mattered went something like this: tell me about your relationship with money – what does it mean to you, how important is it, what did you learn about money as you were growing up? Women revealed their stories to me and together we uncovered their thoughts, feelings and beliefs about money.

More than any other factor, many women fail to get to grips with their finances because their underlying perception of themselves in relation to money is distorted. In such cases practical solutions alone could not help; we also had to tackle the underlying problem.

We have examined a range of emotional responses to money. Now we need to look at how, if left unchecked, those troublesome money emotions can morph into self-limiting money beliefs.

Here are some of the beliefs that our trainee Sheconomists have voiced. How many do you identify with?

- I can't imagine ever feeling really happy until I'm rich
- If I buy that dress it will make me more attractive
- I can't see how saving a few pounds here and there will have any impact on my finances
- Money isn't important to me
- I know that if I have money I will become arrogant, self-satisfied and greedy
- Money stirs up misunderstandings, hurt, confusion and anger

When belief becomes reality

Until the mid-1950s there was widespread belief in the athletics world that a man could not run a mile in under four minutes. Then, in 1954 Roger Bannister notched up his famous world first by running a mile in 3 minutes 59.4 seconds. Was he a one-off super-human? Not at all. That year a further sixteen athletes slammed through the four-minute barrier, too – because they knew, now, it was possible.

The message is this: be open to revising even strongly held beliefs about what's possible. Recognize the self-limiting beliefs that hold you back in life then strive to reach beyond them. Don't be the financial equivalent of a flat-earther. Prepare to overturn preconceptions and commit to Doing Something Different: experience the freedom to enjoy the money you have.

Holding on to self-limiting beliefs is just plain unhelpful to the would-be Sheconomist, as we can see from what Donna told us:

'I grew up with parents who splashed around money they couldn't afford, just to keep up appearances. My mum thought money made you more socially desirable. She thought people judged you by how much you appeared to have. I picked that up from her and, as hard as I try, I can't seem to shake off that attitude.'

This attitude has subsequently informed all Donna's career decisions; it even soured her relationship with a man she might have married. Donna continues:

'I've changed jobs whenever something's come along with a higher salary so I've never really settled anywhere long enough to build up lasting friendships. I'm horrified to think that I even dumped a lovely guy who wanted to marry me. I said it was because I didn't want commitment but truthfully it was because he was a teacher and earned less than me. He didn't have much ambition and drove a clapped out car and I thought I couldn't be with someone like that. I've regretted that in some of my darkest moments.'

At the age of forty-five, Donna's on a six-figure salary and she's one of the highest paid executives in her company yet she hates every minute of her job. She has realized, too late, that her parents' attitude to money was unhelpful to say the least and she's starting to see just how much she's sacrificed for her inherited beliefs.

The seeds of self-limiting beliefs are often sown in childhood or as a result of peer pressure. Such beliefs influence the actions you take, and the actions you *avoid* taking. With their roots in the subconscious you may be unaware of their ill effects upon you: they are like glass walls – you only know they are there when you bump into them. In contrast, when a top Sheconomist says, 'This isn't the way it has to be,' or 'I know I can find a way around this,' we know we're hearing beliefs that can build a better future.

HOW OUR BELIEFS TRIP US UP

Here's an anecdote that exposes how being too fixed in our beliefs or expectations can limit our potential to face reality and solve problems.

Joe and his father were walking along a country road at night when a hit-and-run driver ploughed into them. Joe's father was killed instantly. Joe was rushed to hospital for treatment. Upon seeing him, the hospital surgeon declared: 'That's my son'. How come? Mull this over for a few seconds before you read on . . .

Can't be possible, mistaken identity, you might think, or Joe must have had a step-father. If you ponder the riddle with the subconscious fixed belief that the surgeon must be a man, you'll never solve it. Readjust your man-as-surgeon belief, remember that women (ergo mothers) can be surgeons too and it all falls into place.

Self fulfilling prophecy

The real danger with mistaken money beliefs is that they reflect a false reality, i.e. what we *think* is true. At best they are assumptions – at worst, lies. If we want to, we can trick our brain into believing something good will happen: I will be earning more by this time next year, for example. On the downside, we can become stuck in believing that we are doomed to failure – I'll always be on this lousy salary or me, what chance have I got – and, unless we recognize what's happening and shake off those negative beliefs, the failure may become reality.

Recognizing your money beliefs

This exercise will help identify your money beliefs so that you can decide whether or not they are, in fact, holding you back.

Below are some incomplete statements of belief about

money, read each one aloud to yourself then complete missing parts. Don't spend too long thinking about it. The first thoughts that pop into your head can be the most revealing.

Money is _____

Money isn't _____

If I made more money _____

People that make lots of money are _____

I'm scared that if I have money I will _____

I'm prepared to sacrifice _____ for the sake
   of money

When I think about money, I _____

Having money is _____

I deserve to earn _____

Money symbolises _____

I'm _____ with money

Money is _____

When you've completed the statements read back through them and ask yourself: 'What is the basis of each of those beliefs?'

For example, trainee Sheconomist, Louise, completed the statement 'I'm scared that if I have money I will . . .' with 'let it all slip through my fingers again'. Louise lost £45,000 in the stock market crash and the fall in the housing market in the late eighties, but until she'd completed this exercise she hadn't appreciated how much the experience had left the bad taste of fear in her mouth.

- How far do the beliefs you've expressed in the sentences match your own financial experience to date?
- Always struggling with money? Think about how important it is to you. If you really explore your answer to the 'Money is . . .' question, it may throw up a subconscious dislike of money. Do you believe that people who make piles of money are greedy? Do you believe that being rich means giving up other things in life? If so, this may get in the way of you having a healthy relationship with money

DO SOMETHING DIFFERENT: INCREASE THE FLOW OF MONEY INTO YOUR LIFE

What if your survival depended upon you making extra money?

Set yourself a target sum that you want to make by this time next week – it could be anything, £10, £100 or £1,000. Think of all the possible ways you could go about achieving your target – sorry, illegal ways don't count – and list them.

Here are a few to get you started:

- Put a small ad in the local paper and offer your services for a fee
- Sell stuff on eBay or at a car boot sale
- Become a mystery shopper
- Sell a promise for the future, e.g. give friends a lift to the airport, baby-sit
- Collect all the small change, including foreign currency, from your handbags, behind the sofa, under your car seat, in your desk drawer etc.
- Return unworn clothes and get your money back
- Call in a loan

Chase that money as if your life depended on it. How does it feel? Why not spend more time in future making money rather than spending it? Read the Want to be rich? section later in this chapter.

Look at www.moretolifethanshoes.com Be inspired.

Try this exercise on your own, or ask a friend to do it at the same time and see what you each come up with.

Anna's story

Anna was splitting up from Mark after six years of marriage, some happy, some hideous. Money was just one of the many things she and Mark had argued about, and when she arrived for our first meeting it was clear that Anna had been doing a lot of thinking. I admired her honesty in owning up to the way she had been spending money. 'I love buying clothes,' she told me. 'Especially now I'm finally out of trackie bottoms and don't smell of baby sick. I know I've spent a ridiculous amount.'

The worse the couple's finances got, the more Anna thought 'What the hell' and began to spend more and more frivolously: 'I started to test Mark to see if he'd notice my new highlights or a new dress. When he didn't I thought, "Serves him right".'

I asked Anna if she thought that, as well as using money as a weapon against her husband, there were other reasons for her spending. 'It makes me feel better,' she told me. 'It's been like an anaesthetic to all the pain and sadness.' And the worse her relationship problems had become, the more money Anna had spent: money she now realized she didn't have.

It did not take long to identify the root cause of Anna's overspending: 'My parents were really tight with money – there was never enough to buy me and my brother the things we wanted.

'Whenever anyone gave me some pocket money I'd squirrel it away in my piggy bank and dream of what I could buy. Once, when I was about ten, I opened it to buy a game I wanted. My money had gone and instead I found, of all things, an IOU note from my parents. I was so angry with them.'

And that's when Anna's self-limiting beliefs about money began to take hold. At ten years old, Anna decided that if she ever had children she'd treat them differently. They'd always feel special and loved. She'd buy them nice things even if money was tight. She also decided that saving was pointless. After all, someone could always come and take it away from you.

Anna uncovered more self-limiting beliefs behind her money behaviour, all of which linked back to decisions

she'd made at various points of her life. I asked her to
list them:

- I'm lousy with money
- I deserve nice things
- Buying things compensates for my pain
- Giving presents to my kids demonstrates just how
  much I love them
- It's not safe to have savings
- Being careful with money makes you stingy and
  stops you giving immediate pleasure to those
  around you

When it began to dawn on Anna *why* she was so bad
with money, she was able to begin to take control of
her spending – nothing could have changed without
Anna radically transforming her beliefs about money.

Later in the chapter we'll look at one of her Belief
Busting exercises.

Money would solve all my problems

Do you distract yourself from the day-to-day drudgery of
life by fantasizing about what you'd do with your lottery
winnings? Just that one jackpot and you would jack in
your job tomorrow. If so, you're not alone. But do you
know what? While you are queuing for your lottery ticket
and being let down when the balls don't land for you, life's
real winners are out there, in the *real* world, *making* it
happen.

Of all the self-limiting beliefs, 'I'll get lucky one day' must be the most restricting – a one-way ticket to the Lifetime Non-Achievement Award – and not just because the odds are ludicrously off the planet. Psychological research into the happiness of lottery winners shows it doesn't last, just one year after Bradley Walsh's handshake winners' happiness levels are back where they were before their win. When it comes to making money, the people who achieve lasting happiness are those who have created their own financial success. Wait for luck to deliver your dreams and you miss out on all the buzzy, exhilarating, achievement emotions that make success rewarding.

The chances of you winning the lottery are about fourteen million to one. Compare this with the chances of becoming financially successful under your own steam. The odds must be in your favour. Dreams are wonderful only in the sense that having a positive vision for yourself in the future will propel you down the right path. More about this later . . .

Self-efficacy for Sheconomists

Lots of trainee Sheconomists tell us that they find dealing with money boring or that they don't have the time to manage their money. More often than not, complaints such as these are really excuses for the fact that the trainees don't feel capable of handling their money and related paperwork. This feeling of incapability – a self-limiting belief – often stems from low self-efficacy.

Self-efficacy – a term first coined by psychologist, Albert Bandura – means having a positive belief in your capability to do whatever it is that you set out to do or, to put it another way, to know that you can cope with whatever life throws at you. It's not the same as self-esteem, which concerns how highly you value yourself and which we deal with later.

Check your self-efficacy

Answer yes or no to each of the following six statements:

- I can find the means and ways to manage my money and overcome obstacles that get in my way
- I find it easy to stick to my financial aims and reach my goals
- Unexpected money crises don't bother me – I deal with them efficiently
- When I put in the necessary effort I trust that I can solve any money situation
- I can stay calm when facing money difficulties because I can rely on my coping abilities
- When faced with a financial problem, I can usually come up with several solutions

(adapted from Jerusalem & Schwatzer 1981)

How did you do? If you said yes to all six statements then

you have amazing self-efficacy and are well on your way to becoming a top Sheconomist. Congratulations.

If you said yes to fewer than six, don't worry, this isn't unusual, but it does reveal the extent of your belief in your ability to be an effective operator in the finance arena. It's likely that you think money-related tasks are harder than they actually are. If that is the case, start to explore ways in which you could challenge this belief.

First, accept that managing money really isn't *that* difficult. The financial world and all the fancy jargon they use tends to alienate women – and girls are often given the message that they're not cut out for numbers, so we start off feeling disadvantaged – but really it is much easier than they'd have us imagine.

Whatever our destiny, the one thing we are all going to encounter in our lives is money yet the subject is conspicuously absent from virtually every school curriculum. Little wonder, then, that we emerge from years in the classroom not knowing our assets from our elbows. But remember, you do not need a PhD in applied maths to deal with personal finance. Far from it.

It's a common myth that you have to be good at maths to manage your money. Modern technology has come to the rescue of the numerically challenged: find help with working out budgets on www.sheconomics.com or keep track of day-to-day spending by downloading a budgeting tool such as www.creditaction.org.uk/spendometer.html directly onto a mobile phone.

Fed up being underpaid?

Loads of women tell us that overspending is their problem. It's a problem the rest would love to have. They barely earn enough to survive, let alone to splurge.

One trainee Sheconomist told us she was always just a bill or two away from debt. When an accountant pointed out her minuscule profit margins – based on the time she was putting in, her hourly rate was actually less than the minimum wage – it hit her that she was woefully under-charging for her services. Like many self-employed women, and despite being highly talented, she shied away from asking for what she was really worth.

And women are far more likely to under-earn than men. There is a whole host of reasons for this: most feel useless at negotiating their way through pay structures and asking for a rise; many organizations persist in the archaic tradition of paying women less than men – and, yes, they're still getting away with it – and more women than men take jobs that will fit around their children's needs, so they often accept lower pay in return for flexibility.

Whether you 'under-earn' depends on where you set your benchmark. What's a living wage to one woman might be a windfall to another, but just make sure you don't set your benchmark too low. And remember, money doesn't have the foggiest idea which sex you are.

ARE YOU AN UNDER-EARNER?

Here are some questions (adapted from Barbara Stanny's book *Overcoming Underearning*) to help you spot whether or not you are an under-earner. Answer yes or no:

1. Do you avoid asking for a pay rise or putting up your prices?

2. Do you work very hard for little money?

3. Would you think it unfair for you to earn a high income if other people work harder for less money?

4. Do you often give away your time for free, do jobs for people or put in extra time at work, for no extra pay?

5. Do you find it hard to think of ideas to make money?

6. Are you often in debt with no idea how you'll achieve financial success?

7. Are you proud of the fact that you can manage on less money than most?

8. Does the idea of having lots of money make you feel uncomfortable or fearful?

9. Do you live in financial chaos, with little or no idea what you earn, spend and what debt you have?

10. Do you think that people who seek wealth are greedy?

If you answered yes to three or more of the questions you are likely to be an under-earner. Your pay simply doesn't match your potential. Maybe you justify it by telling yourself that you don't deserve more. Perhaps you take pride in rejecting the trappings of wealth. At some level you may be pushing money away from you.

Now, if you have identified yourself as an under-earner, ask yourself whether you've subconsciously imposed limits on what you can earn. The good news is that you can raise the threshold – it's all about how to be less 'I'm not worth that much money' and more 'I deserve a higher salary'. The next DSD exercise is designed to help you shed your self-imposed limits and allow more money to flow into your life.

DO SOMETHING DIFFERENT: KNOW WHAT YOU'RE WORTH

You know you should be earning more. But your subconscious – the part of your mind that generates those self-limiting beliefs – keeps tripping you up. This exercise helps you to believe that you're worth whatever you want to earn.

Take yourself off into a room alone for five minutes. Then, say out loud the amount you want to earn. It's important to actually speak, rather than just think. Shout out your ideal annual salary, your anticipated profits or your daily or hourly rate.

Maybe you're aiming for a salary of £60,000. Start by saying, 'I earn sixty thousand pounds a year'. Then double it and say, 'I earn a hundred and twenty thousand pounds a year'. Then keep doubling it again and again, until you reach a ridiculous salary that only David Beckham is familiar with.

When you reach that silly figure, practise saying aloud that you earn this whopping amount. Keep it up until you can say it in a neutral way, just as you'd reel off your phone number. This tricks your subconscious into believing what you're saying.

Then, when you talk to your manager about the pay rise or higher daily rate you actually want, it'll seem to you like peanuts. You will come across with real conviction. Why? Because you'll believe that's what you're worth.

Want to be rich?

Stop for a moment and visualize a typical millionaire. Do you see a tanned, Armani-suited man, his wife dripping in diamonds, being chauffeur-driven to their luxury yacht where a posse of servants wait to tend their every need?

In *The Millionaire Next Door* authors Thomas Stanley and William Danko explode the myths about 'typical' millionaires. In their research they questioned hundreds of mega-rich men (now there's a good job!) and, surprisingly, they found that the male millionaire looks more like the bloke next door than Rockefeller. He's likely to drive an older car and he probably doesn't possess a single item of designer clothing. They'll be telling us next he has a jar of pennies under his bed and lives with his mum! But the fact is, one reason the typical millionaire has so much money is he tends to be frugal with it. Not only that, the authors' research showed that, if he's married, his wife will be a meticulous budgeter and definitely more Primark than Prada.

What about female millionaires, you ask? In *Millionaire Women Next Door,* Dr Stanley found they weren't wallowing in champagne and couldn't care less about appearing loaded: 'In fact,' writes Stanley, 'an enhanced-consumption lifestyle is very low on their list of the benefits of becoming wealthy. They have discovered that happiness can be achieved – and, actually, greatly enhanced – without their becoming hyperconsumers.' Brings a whole new meaning to cheap and cheerful. So our beliefs about millionaires are wide of the mark.

Most of them have concentrated on accumulating wealth, not spending it – or showing it.

Spotted your self-limiting beliefs yet?

OK, time to remove the blinkers. Prompted by what you've read so far, you have probably felt one or two of your self-limiting beliefs bubbling to the surface. But in case you haven't, here's a list of some of the beliefs that hold women back. Circle any that resonate with you and add any of your own at the end.

Changing your beliefs

You need money to make money	Money is the root of all evil
I'm not special enough to be well-off	You should never borrow money
I can't save	It's lonely at the top
It's impossible to make a lot of money doing a job you enjoy	I'm ignorant about money so I probably get ripped off without even knowing it
I can't control my spending	Money isn't important to me
I can't attract money into my life	I'm useless with money
What's the point in making any more money, the government will take it all anyway	The wealthy think that they're superior to everyone else
These days, debt is just a part of life	Wealth symbolizes success

Money changes people for the worse	I'll never have enough money to retire
I find anything to do with finance deadly boring	You can never have too much insurance
You only get paid well if you suffer	If I became rich I may not like myself
Never trust anyone offering financial advice	Money would sort out all of my problems
If the worst comes to the worst, my parents could bail me out	What's the point of saving for retirement – I may not live that long
It's better to be safe than sorry	I must never have any debt
I don't have enough money to save	You get what you pay for
Now write down any of your own below:	

Ever had a disagreement with someone about politics? Then you'll know that belief change isn't simple. Nevertheless, what you are aiming for here is to change a belief that, deep down, you know is not serving you well. We're now at the point where you have identified your beliefs and, therefore, you're ready to go beyond them.

Here's what we suggest you do. Three simple steps. Trust us, it gets easier with practice:

1. Take one of your negative beliefs. Think about where it came from, and how it affects what you do.
2. Next, replace it by turning it into the opposite, positive belief. Consider how you'd feel if this positive belief was true.

3. Finally, think of how you could reinforce the positive belief, i.e. what would you actually do? Commit to taking some concrete steps towards making this happen.

Here's a working example:

Let's say you're battling with a negative 'I'm no good with money' belief. To this end, you avoid anything even vaguely related to finance.

Replace it with its positive: 'I'm great with money'. Then consider how you'd feel if this positive belief was true.

How would you reinforce this new 'I'm great with money' belief? You might research some courses in financial management, or set up a review meeting with your bank manager or financial advisor, or reorganize all your paperwork into neat and tidy files, or list your financial goals to achieve this year.

Getting the idea?
Make sure you word your new beliefs positively, so that you say explicitly what you *will* do, not what you *won't* do. For

example, instead of saying 'I *won't* overspend' say 'I *will* save fifty pounds every month'. Then focus on the goal. And try not to think too much about your old, self-limiting behaviour – psychologist Dr James Erskine showed that the more we think about something we're trying not to do, the more chance we will do it; he calls it behavioural rebound.

When trying to change your beliefs, a common stumbling block is all-or-nothing thinking. Make sure your language isn't littered with absolutes. For example, saying to yourself, 'I *know* I'll *never* get onto the property ladder'. Here, 'know' is very limiting and 'never' is, well, hopeless – both words are sure-fire barriers to action. But replace 'I know' with 'I wonder' and you've opened the door to possibilities: 'I wonder if I could get on the property ladder?'. After saying it a few times the action that follows might be to view a flat. Seeing a property and feeling the excitement of perhaps owning your own home could motivate you to budget and save.

Another language trap to watch out for is the 'Yes, but . . .' response – avoid it, it's limiting because it, also, reflects that 'can't do' mindset.

Below are ten of our top, positive, Sheconomic beliefs. Do try to develop your own, though – positive beliefs tailored to challenge whichever negative you've identified as your biggest obstacle to action.

Ten Top Positive Sheconomic Beliefs

- Money matters as much as health or relationships in my life
- Money is neither good nor bad. It has no intrinsic meaning
- I deserve to have the financial security and lifestyle I want
- There's enough money to go round
- I create the results in my life
- I'm grateful for the money that flows into my life
- I can increase my knowledge about money and finance
- I'm a money magnet
- It's easier to make money than to spend it
- I can be well off and a good person at the same time

Just imagine how great you'd feel if you adopted all ten. Try repeating some of them aloud to yourself and get a taste for the power of positive thinking.

Belief busting

In Anna's story, earlier in the chapter, Anna came up with quite a mix of self-limiting beliefs: I'm lousy with money; I deserve nice things; buying things compensates for my pain; giving presents to my kids demonstrates just how much I love them; it's not safe to have savings; being careful with money makes you greedy and stops you giving immediate pleasure to those around you.

Once she'd identified her beliefs and how they were linked to her money troubles she really set to work on them. As well as having a go at the techniques we've just described, Anna kept a belief busting log – writing down her self-limiting beliefs, then countering them with some sparkly new positive ones.

Read Anna's account then write your own log.

What self-limiting belief do you hold about money?	ANNA'S ANSWERS I know I'm lousy with money.
How did this belief arise?	I've had no savings, only debt, since Mark and I first got together. Mum's always nagging me to take better control of my money, yet she's no better. I wonder if this is actually about me not being worthy of having money?
What do you do to reinforce this belief?	I've stopped opening my bank statements; I just don't want to know the bad stuff. I make myself feel better by spending on the kids. I never really work out where my money goes. I feel I'm being selfish if I say no to the kids.

Describe the opposite, positive belief and put it in the present tense, e.g. 'I am completely in control of my money'.	I manage my money well – never spending more than I can afford and I have enough put away for the future.
How would you feel if you had this new positive belief?	I'd stop feeling constantly stressed out about money. I'd feel I've got a better future ahead of me. I'd feel proud of myself and no longer feel like I've let down my parents. And I'd feel like a good mum to my kids.
How would you change your behaviour to reinforce this positive belief?	I would open up my bank statements and sort out a budget so I only spend what I can afford. I would find other ways of showing the kids love. I would ask my friends for support. And turn off the telly and get down to sorting out my debts and making a savings plan.
What actions can you commit to now, to support the new positive belief?	I'll change the way I talk about money. I'll sort out a realistic plan for spending and give myself a budget for fun spending. I'll talk to a friend about maybe meeting each week to help each other control our money. I'll stick a list on the fridge of ways of showing the kids love that don't involve money. I'll talk to the kids about a monthly allowance that we can't exceed. And I'll plan some affordable days out with the kids. And I'll tell myself I'm good with money!

Now it's your turn: refer back to the self-limiting beliefs table, look at those you circled, select the one you'd most like to topple and fill in the log below.

You can complete the log on your own, but do it with your partner or a friend and you could brainstorm more positive thoughts and actions together.

If you find this helpful, fill in the log for each of the self-limiting beliefs you circled earlier.

Belief Busting Log	
What self-limiting belief do you hold about money?	
How did this belief arise?	
What do you do to reinforce this belief?	
Describe the opposite, positive belief and put it in the present tense, e.g. 'I am completely in control of my money'.	
How would you feel if you had this new positive belief?	
How would you change your behaviour to reinforce this positive belief?	
What actions can you commit to now, to support the new positive belief?	

It's all in your mind

For any of you who might still be sceptical about whether changing your beliefs about money really can change your attitude and behaviour towards it, we have scientific proof from two Dutch psychologists, Dijksterhui and van Knippenbereg, who performed this fascinating experiment.

They asked two groups of people to think themselves into two different roles, football hooligans and university professors. Then each person in each group had to write down everything they could think of connected with their assigned role. Both groups were asked forty-two *Trivial Pursuit* questions. Those who'd imagined they were professors beat the imaginary football hooligans hands-down – yet the two groups had the same intelligence quotients.

Sadly, we can't permanently raise our IQs by thinking we're Einstein but, as this experiment demonstrates, what we believe when we approach a situation can, and does, influence the outcome. Think about that next time you go to ask your bank manager for a loan.

Now, try acting 'as if . . .' and see how it can improve your money beliefs:

- Pick one of your less positive money beliefs
- Jot down how it affects your behaviour

- Ask yourself, 'If I knew this belief was untrue, how would I act?'
- Experiment by acting 'as if' your belief was untrue

Try on a different money mindset with the DSD exercise below.

DO SOMETHING DIFFERENT: ACT LIKE A PRINCESS OR A PAUPER

Act the opposite of how you would normally when it comes to money – just for a day!

If you're normally on a tight budget and very cautious with your money, act as if you're fantastically wealthy and profligate. Dress up and go to the supermarket – imagine you're an A-list celebrity the paparazzi may be waiting to snap. Test drive a car you can't afford, browse around a ridiculously expensive jewellers, tell at least one person to 'keep the change' – even if it's only what's left out of a fiver after you've spent £4.99!

Think rich, feel rich. Is wealth really a matter of money or more a state of mind?

Maybe we've just described you on a normal day? In that case, act as if you are totally strapped for cash. Look for the cheapest bargain on everything you buy, count the pennies in your purse and see if you can scrape together enough for a bite of lunch. Walk or take public transport instead of driving your car.

Does all this make you more aware of money than you are normally?

Before we move on, let's recap on the Sheconomics law **Go beyond beliefs:**

• You've identified and analysed your self-limiting beliefs.

• You're ready to change your behaviour and attitude towards money that you can see will have a pay-off for you.

• You are feeling more financially free.

My Sheconomics Checklist
Law 2

Are you going beyond your beliefs? If you can tick all the boxes you're well on the way ✓

I know that some of my beliefs limit me	
I won't be tricked into believing a belief is the truth	
I won't let self-limiting beliefs get in the way of my financial success	
I have a whole set of shiny new positive beliefs	
I'll reinforce new beliefs by taking action	
I'll try to Do Something Different whenever I spot a self-limiting belief	

Chapter 4
Law 3: Spend with power

> Annual income twenty pounds, annual
> expenditure nineteen nineteen six, result
> happiness. Annual income twenty pounds,
> annual expenditure twenty pounds ought
> and six, result misery.
>
> Charles Dickens (author)

Do you ever spend money you don't have? On things you
don't need? Perhaps even to impress people you don't
know? Only to find yourself no happier?

Why?

Shopping can, of course, be a fabulous experience – and
who doesn't love gorgeous things? But from the moment
we enter a shop we are in danger: the music, the colours,
the offers, even the way the clothes are hung – all
cunningly designed to separate us from our money. Don't
get the wrong idea: we're not anti shopping, we're anti
feeling-bad-after-shopping. We are dead against the you-
are-what-you-own messages propagated by the
consumer society.

We're not going to ask you to stop shopping. We do, however, want you to understand why you shop and, if need be, help you cut down in ways that won't leave you feeling deprived – our list of alternative therapies at the end of the chapter will ensure that. Yes, it *is* possible to have treats galore without draining the bank balance.

Feeling taken for granted, boredom and dissatisfaction with life, among other things, can all lead to overdependence on shopping. With a heady mix including demanding jobs and families, long working hours and multiple roles to juggle plus a 'because I'm worth it' culture, women feel they should have more treats. And the rewards needn't be huge, as one trainee Sheconomist told us:

'Even supermarket shopping gives me a huge buzz. I'll buy a face cream or some DVDs to "treat myself". It's justified because it comes out of the groceries' budget.'

OK, a few DVDs probably never set anyone on the rocky road to destitution. Many women, however, tell us they feel powerless when it comes to spending – and that they are spending more than they earn. We are going to help you build up the power you need to resist your own compulsions and pressures such as marketing ploys – the power to walk away from the till. Not only that, you'll be able to use your money to enhance your life instead of using it to compensate for something that's missing in it.

We asked more than 700 women about their spending in the previous seven days. Sixty per cent had bought something on impulse. Almost half the women had succumbed to a special offer. A third had parted with more money than they could afford, almost as many had bought something they would probably never wear or use. Almost half confessed to going out for one thing but coming back with something completely different – you know, when you pop out for a pint of milk and come back with a flat-screen TV. More than three-quarters confessed to using shopping as a way of cheering themselves up but, sadly, for lots of them it had the opposite effect.

When you spend with power you'll be able to:

- Resist compulsions to spend to cover up emotions
- Confront your spending patterns
- Spend less than you earn
- Create a spending plan so you can recognize when your finances start moving in the wrong direction
- Discover that the good things in life don't necessarily cost money

Resisting pressure

Take the media obsession with celebrity and aspirational lifestyles. It's all hugely entertaining but it doesn't make us feel better about ourselves. In fact, it can leave us feeling totally inadequate. Only got four colour-coordinated cushions on your satin-encased bed? Don't you know it's *de rigueur* to have *at least* twelve? What were you thinking?

These days it seems as though everyone's trying to wheedle their way into your wallet. So, unless you keep a tight-fisted grip on your money, it has a nasty habit of slipping through your fingers. Advertisers not only make you aware of your problems, they also offer the solution: shopping. It's a tough world for any woman who feels unfulfilled. What's your weakness? Unhappy with your looks? Relationship troubles? Fighting depression?

Look at what the advertisers are telling you: go on, you deserve it; smart girls get more; it's not about what you need, it's about what you want. One of many devious ploys involves telling women they 'deserve' whatever it is that they desire. We are being seduced by a false entitlement fantasy, a false promise, and we're meant to think: 'I'm worth it, so I must be entitled to it'. We're persuaded to buy, whether or not we have the money.

No matter how great it feels to lavish money on yourself, there's no way on earth any handbag, moisturizing serum or those nail extensions are going to help you feel emotionally in charge. Spending with power means knowing you have choices. And the option to firmly reject what's being tantalizingly dangled before you.

The retail industry is huge and its influence is far reaching. In the UK women spend more than £13 billion a year on clothes alone – that's twice as much as men and much of that expenditure is funded by debt.

Most women wear just 10 per cent of their clothes 90 per cent of the time, which adds up to an awful lot of wardrobes groaning with rarely – or never-worn buying blunders. More than half of all women have something in the wardrobe with the shop's label still on it. More to the point, while we are jostling with the sales crowds, queuing for a changing cubicle or selecting soft furnishings, our male counterparts are buying houses and checking out the best investment opportunities.

Recent research by market analysts Mintel described Britain as 'a nation of unashamed big spenders'. Fuelled by a fascination with image and lifestyle, consumer spending in 2006 rocketed to a record 1.09 trillion pounds. The research also showed that big spenders were putting their lifestyle spending before other financial commitments, including those all-important credit card repayments.

Spending with power means being able to balance a great quality of life with a degree of financial responsibility. *Boring* we hear you cry. But you can, in fact, have a positive, fun-filled life and also pay your bills.

How to achieve this? A crucial first step is to have high self-esteem. When it comes to shopping, it's the women with low self-esteem who lose control and buckle under the pressures. Research shows that compulsive buyers have lower self-esteem than any other type of shopper. But when you feel strong within yourself you won't be easily manipulated and you'll be able to stand up to the brand bullies.

Style counsel

The fashion world bangs on about the current season's look, then the fashion police pour scorn on anyone with the nerve to think they can get away with wearing it next season. If something looks good on you, why shouldn't you wear it? Bay Garnett, author of *The Cheap Date Guide to Style*, is horrified by the 'sheep mentality' with which women follow fast fashion, 'knocking each other over to get cheap clothes in Primark'. Many of these hard-won purchases will be worn at most once or twice before the owner decides they're yesterday's news, which makes you wonder how good-value they really are!

I (Karen) have a penchant for clothes from designers who only produce a few wacky pieces per collection. They're not cheap but I adore them and get tons of wear from them. Some I've had for ten years or more so the big price tag is justified on a cost-per-wear basis.

If you have fashion-victim tendencies ask your friends to be open and honest about what looks good on you. Once you've recovered from their comments, you can focus on developing a wardrobe of clothes that flatter. Keep it simple, less really is more when it comes to style and try to select clothes that will stand the test of time. Aim to rise above the pressure to conform. Clothes are a medium for self-expression, but be careful not to mortgage yourself to the whims of a fickle fashion industry. Be choosy about who you shop with, too. Watch out for friends who enjoy egging you on to spend money but never seem to part with their own.

Don't give in to temptation
Shopping for clothes shouldn't take priority over the other good things in life, yet many women say they prefer shopping to sex – sadly, a trolley dash in Top Shop would be their choice. One trainee Sheconomist even admitted that she rewards herself with clothes shopping:

> *'Some of us lie back and think of England, I lie back and think about shopping.'*

Next time you're bagging yet another pair of skinny jeans – you know, the ones Kate Moss was wearing in last week's *Grazia* – use the DSD questions below to wake up to reality. If you answer yes to *any* of the questions, muster the power of resistance, put whatever you were about to bag right back on the rail and walk away.

DO SOMETHING DIFFERENT: HONE YOUR DISCERNING BUYING SKILLS

Before you head for the till, ask yourself:

- Is it a high cost item and 'hot' at the moment?
- Are you in two minds about whether it really suits you?
- Does it draw attention to parts of your body you should really play down?
- Will it only go with one or two other items in your wardrobe?
- Do you *like* rather than *love* it?
- Would you actually prefer it if it was in another colour?
- Be honest – do you want it just so you can wear something new tonight?
- If it's reduced in the sale, are you buying it just because it's a bargain and something you wouldn't buy at the full price?

Remember – ONE yes answer means you should PUT IT BACK.

Go on, you'll thank us for it, some day.

A symptom of our decadent society is that we quickly tire of even the most gorgeous clothes in our wardrobe. Most of us have more than we need, yet new garb still has a seductive allure. One trainee Sheconomist described a feeling common to many:

'I spend all my disposable income and buy clothes every single weekend – but still I never seem to have anything to wear!'

Safe in the knowledge that today's 'can't resist it' will be tomorrow's 'that old thing', here are some no-spend ways to get the thrill of the new:

1. Try swapping instead of shopping: someone might covet the clutter you've tired of and be willing to swap.
2. Find a dressmaker: if you have the perfect dress/skirt/pair of trousers, have the style copied in summer and winter fabrics.
3. Sort, pack and store clothes away at the end of each season: in spring, for example, dry clean (and repair if necessary) woollies and winter heavy fabrics. Give away, bin or sell any you haven't worn for a year. Pack the rest away – lovingly. You can buy large PVC garment bags from hardware stores. Put tissue paper between garments, add sprigs of lavender to keep them fresh and to deter moths. When cooler weather returns you'll enjoy bringing those clothes out again. If you chose them carefully in the first place and bought great cut and quality, they'll be just as exciting as any new buys.

DO SOMETHING DIFFERENT: NO PURCHASE NECESSARY

Leave your money at home for a day.

Make sure you've got some food with you, that there's petrol in the car and credit on your mobile. Then experience the feeling of going out without a penny in your pocket. Many people the world over do this once a year on Buy Nothing Day – have a look at www.buynothingday.co.uk.

Discover as many ways as you can of enjoying yourself for free.

Visit museums or art galleries that don't charge admission, join a TV or radio show audience, snap up a free or discarded newspaper or magazine on the train. Rediscover your legs – walk or cycle instead of driving or using public transport.

For lots more free events and attractions go to www.dofreestuff.co.uk or www.afreedayout.co.uk

For free stuff (anything from a flip phone to a camping trailer), join a free recycling group www.freecycle.org.

Consumer confidence

Don't forget that as a consumer you have rights; have the confidence to exert them. We hate being ripped off, yet women are notoriously weak when it comes to doing anything about it. For example, don't pay the restaurant service charge when the service is poor and do return shoddy goods. And when did you last negotiate the best possible deal on your mobile phone or service contracts?

As a general rule, resist extended warranties on goods and turn down free trial periods – you're almost bound to end up paying for something you'll neither use nor want.

Controlling your habits

In our survey, a whopping 79 per cent of women said they would spend less than they currently do if they had more self-control. Be honest, how much does shopping feature in your life?

An airline questionnaire listed shopping as a hobby. We believe shopping has become more habit than hobby and, sadly, for many of us the shopping habit has replaced our hobbies. What the psychologist terms 'spending styles' we call spending habits.

The shopping habits below are all examples of ways that we women give away our spending power.

- **Competitive spending** Keeping up with the Joneses matters to you. You want to build an image, gain status and need to have what others have. You've been known to buy things just to out-do someone else. You need to keep up with others in a conspicuous way.

- **Compulsive spending** Your spending is emotionally driven; often because of poor quality relationships. For you, shopping takes the place of affection, fulfilment or other rewards that are missing from your life. In some cases it can even be a way of punishing yourself. You tend to spend impulsively when you're depressed, lonely or upset.

- **Narcissistic spending** Looking good is important to you and you believe you're entitled to have whatever you want. You believe you'll be judged by your appearance. As you shop, you fantasize about winning admiring glances from others. You are fascinated by fame and celebrity – feelings of inferiority may be at the root of this.

- **Bargain spending** Your home is so cluttered with bargain buys, special offers and bulk purchases that you can never find anything. The triumph of seizing what you think is an offer too good to miss gives you justification to overspend. You kid yourself you're saving money but, in reality, you're a soft touch when it comes to the hard sell.

- **Co-dependent spending** You spend lavishly on others. This may be with the intention of keeping them dependent and close. You may buy things for others to compensate for not spending enough time with them, or spend money to elevate yourself in your friends' eyes – not having the strength to say 'no'. You may wish to control another person or feel you have to spend money on them because you can't meet their emotional needs.

- **Revenge spending** You spend the money of a loved one as a means of punishing them. If they are spending recklessly, you think it gives you the right to do so too. You may be getting back at them because of something they did wrong in the past. You may be reacting against someone's insensitivity, lack or appreciation of you or lack of attention towards you.

If you have recognized any of your spending habits here, don't despair, Sheconomics has the solution. It's impossible to go from Big Spender to Top Sheconomist overnight. First, you need to get to the root of why you're spending the way you are now and that's where the first two laws of Sheconomics come in: to help you identify, take control of and change those negative money emotions and self-limiting beliefs. Come to grips with those first two laws and begin to set yourself financially free to start spending with power.

We each have our own ways of coping under pressure – and most of the time, most of us deal perfectly well with the knocks life inevitably brings. Sometimes, however, some of us feel the need to seek solace in ways which are ultimately damaging – starving or bingeing on food, abusing drugs or alcohol, compulsive gambling and, of course, compulsive shopping – so commonly used by women.

To the women who do it, being known as a compulsive shopper feels, somehow, less shameful than, say, being known as an alcoholic. Overspending on clothes does not attract the same stigma as overdosing on drugs. It's even acceptable to admit you enjoy overspending. And it's enormously rewarding at the time – as indeed are the abuser's drug, drink, bet, and so on.

Habitual overspending is, however, a problem and the more ingrained any habit becomes, the more difficult it becomes to exercise the willpower to curb it. As one trainee Sheconomist told us:

'If I'm experiencing any kind of emotional pain I spend, spend, spend. The last time a boyfriend broke up with me I racked up about a thousand pounds in a few weeks. I have enormous debt brought on through years of spending this way.'

Lara's story

Lara worked for a large charity and described her job as high-powered and exciting. 'But there are days when the constant demands, the pressure and the stress just leave me ready to scream,' she admitted.

Over the years, Lara had come to realize that her 'down' days could be treated very effectively with a large injection of retail therapy – it made her feel better, albeit temporarily. After a bad day at work she always went shopping. Sometimes she treated herself to a glamorous top, a handbag or a snazzy accessory, other times it was all these things and more. Lara's shopping habit had got way out of hand; she was stacking up debt and she'd once spent more than £1,000 in a high street fashion store in less than fifteen minutes.

In the immediate aftermath of one shopping spree Lara's guilt and shame were palpable. 'I just don't know how it happens,' she told me. She described her thoughts as she walked towards the shops: 'I tell myself that I've worked hard so I deserve it. After all, I've spent all day giving to others, why shouldn't I give myself a little something? Otherwise, what's the point of working?'

Lara's shopping habit was her automatic, unplanned reaction to stress at work. She felt powerless to resist even though she was running into debt. Lara needed to realize that shopping was not her route to happiness. She needed to Do Something Different.

As she racked up more debt, her dream of buying her own flat was rapidly dwindling. She wasn't proud of herself. When she thought of the rising pile of purchases she was hoarding, she felt sick. Eventually Lara realized that it was time to act rather than fret about a problem that wouldn't go away by itself. See page 93 for how she took control of her spending.

There is terminology aplenty to describe Lara's habitual overspending: shopaholic, addictive-buying behaviour, compulsive acquisition disorder; Professor Lorrin Karan from Stanford University would call it impulse control disorder while Jeffrey Schaler, author of *Addiction Is a Choice* believes such disorders and syndromes are nothing but irresponsible behaviour under a fancy name. Ultimately, the labels don't really help. We'd say Lara had a shopping habit, a pattern that is probably recognizable to many women, and was powerless in the face of it.

Get a grip on spending

We've seen how hard it can be to resist the pull of the
shops, and how hard it is to turn your back on the very
thing that will perk you up when you're feeling low. But it's
important to try, and doing something different in order to
distract yourself from your habitual response is a smart
way to fight your reaction to overspend .

If you have trouble controlling your spending, these five
simple tips will help to put the power back in your hands:

- **Take only cash**
  Decide in advance how much you can afford to spend
  when you go on a shopping trip. Take that amount in
  cash and leave your credit cards at home.

- **Shop alone**
  Shopping with friends usually leads to you spending
  more – you may be persuaded to buy something you
  don't really like or want. Shop alone or, if you need to
  shop with someone, choose your companion carefully.

- **Change your plans**
  If one day of the weekend has become a regular
  shopping day, plan other activities for that day. Fun
  things that don't take you near the shops or involve
  overspending.

- **A small treat does the trick**

  If you really can't bear to go home empty handed, indulge yourself with a tiny, inexpensive treat – your favourite flowers, a soothing foot soak, an enticing novel.

- **Only shop when you're in good shape**

  Never shop when you're hungry or unhappy. Hunger is guaranteed to make you fill your basket with the wrong type of food. And when emotions are high, rationality goes out the window and you're more likely to make the wrong purchasing decisions.

Here's one of our trainee Sheconomists on this subject:

  'I have to try and avoid going shopping when I've been feeling bad about myself because I spend money I don't need to spend, or can't afford. I know it gives me just a short high followed by a deeper 'down' . . . a kind of emptiness, swiftly followed by the guilt of knowing how stupid it was.'

Beat addictive tendencies

Compulsive shoppers – and they come from all walks of life – tell us they find themselves thinking: 'Did I really spend that much yesterday?' A shopping binge can bring on a horrible spending hangover. Lots of women tell us their shopping euphoria is followed by a profound sense of emotional emptiness. The effect on their bank accounts aside, they plummet into feelings of hollow regret, guilt and shame – and how do they relieve these feelings? By going shopping.

When we use the word addiction in relation to shopping or spending, it's important to bear in mind that we're talking about psychological, not physical, dependence. A heroin or alcohol addict for example is physically dependent on their drug, the shopper or gambler is psychologically dependent on spending and betting respectively. Psychological research shows that many women go on spending sprees to fill an emotional void within themselves, or to overcome their frustration at not getting what they want from life: it's called compensatory consumption. For women such as these, spending becomes an escape route from personal problems. We cover this in our chapter on taking emotional control.

Women locked in compensatory consumption give money a power it doesn't have. But it does *not* have the power to solve problems, it is simply a means of exchange. Nonetheless, the emotional high that compulsive spenders get from shopping is enough to keep them hooked even though, not surprisingly, they feel let down in the end. Shopaholics describe physical symptoms including raised pulse rate, hyperventilation alongside psychological symptoms including an inability to walk away and a sense of euphoria as they make a purchase. Ask an addicted gambler how they feel when they place a bet and the sensations will match.

This response is the result of the brain's natural reaction when it anticipates a reward. Put simply, the brain's 'pleasure circuits' become activated, a chemical called dopamine is released and, ultimately, this triggers the physical and emotional symptoms we describe as a thrill or excitement – and people can get 'addicted' to the high. But after the high comes the crushing low – the shame over crippling debts, guilt about all the unopened shopping bags under the bed. This, so often, is what has sent so many women in search of professional help.

A lot of people overspend from time to time but any problems such occasional expenditure might throw up are, in general, soon fixed. The compulsive shopper will persist in her psychological addiction to spend regardless of the consequences – debt, family break-up, emotional breakdown, whatever.

You may or may not know if you have a problem with overspending. Are you reading this and thinking 'That's me!' – whether you are or not, we urge you to complete our Am I Addicted? questionnaire:

AM I ADDICTED?

If you are worried that you may have a serious problem and it's getting out of control, these questions (adapted from addictions.co.uk) will help you decide whether you need further advice or help.

- Do you regularly spend more than you can afford?
- Does your spending ever cause upset to your friends or family?
- Do other people tell you that your spending is a problem or out of control?
- Are you more likely to spend compulsively when you feel low?
- Does going shopping when you're low or feeling overwhelmed lift your mood?
- Do you often find that you spend far more than you initially intended to?
- Do you ever feel that you can't stop yourself spending once you have started?
- Do you experience negative emotions after a spending spree (shame, remorse, guilt, self-hatred, a sense of hopelessness)?
- Have you ever spent money in order to try to get rid of your negative emotions?
- Have you ever, unsuccessfully, tried to seriously cut back on your spending for any length of time?
- Has your spending problem or debt ever made you think about ending your life?
- Do you carry on spending even though you're still coping with the consequences of previous episodes; i.e. adding to already high debts?

Did you answer yes to more than three of the questions? Then it's time to confront the seriousness of your problem.

When negative emotions lead to spending and spending leads to euphoria then self-loathing, it's time to seek help. You could talk to your GP or seek out a coach or therapist who might help you address whatever issues are at the root of your problem, such as low self-esteem or relationship difficulties.

Delay gratification

Young children want instant gratification. Ask a three year-old if she'd like one sweet now or the whole packet tomorrow – she'll take one sweet now. But an adult who is offered £1 now or £10 in a month would usually exercise enough self-control to hold out for the £10. We do all give in to the odd infantile quest for momentary pleasure now and again and the occasional lapse of self-control is fine. If such lapses become habitual and excessive – be it to do with drinking, eating, spending – lives can be wrecked.

DO SOMETHING DIFFERENT: LEARN TO SAY NO

- Practise saying No to your demanding inner child and to others.
- Do you prefer to spend your money on an instantly gratifying treat rather than invest and earn a bit of interest on it?
- Next time you're tempted to indulge, just say 'No'.
- Don't think of it as deprivation, turn it around and see it as a way of wielding power.
- Happiness does not depend on trinkets and designer labels.

Spending with power involves keeping the hedonistic, pleasure-seeking parts of our brain in check. Research from the newly emerging field of neuroeconomics shows that spending decisions are a trade-off between the pleasure and the pain regions of the brain.

In experiments looking at the effects of spending on the brain, Brian Knutson of Stanford University in the US found that, when people are weighing up whether to buy something and how much to pay for it, their brain scans revealed a 'hedonic competition between the immediate pleasure of acquisition and the equally immediate pain of paying'. So that's why the Buy Now, Pay Later deals are so tempting.

We live in a world where we're told we should never have to wait for anything. We can have all the pleasure now and put off the pain until later. Buy that sofa you adore today and just hope you still love it five years hence when you have to start paying for it. Credit cards are a dangerous way of delaying the pain – they should be called debt cards.

Once you can spend with power you start to make the right choices in life – saying 'yes' to some things, while happily giving others the big N-O. The economist Ross Gittins says the power lies in the realization that we have 'present selves' and 'long-run selves'. Your present self is the instant gratifier, the one that screams, 'Have it! Now, now, now!' It only cares about today and thinks nothing of blowing out on the credit card and passing on the costs to your 'long-run self.' The delaying long-run self – that's the sensible bit – knows all about the advantages of waiting, of holding off spending today in exchange for wealth and security in the future.

Many of the women we've spoken to tell us that their present selves always win when it comes to their passion for shoes and handbags. That's when bills don't even get a look in. We've come across loads of women with a serious shoe habit that extends to literally hundreds of pairs. The transformative power of shoes must be what appeals – you can go from drudge to seductress in seconds. How about that for instant gratification?

But if the next pair of killer heels could push your bank balance into the red here's a DSD that will switch on the sensible part of your brain.

DO SOMETHING DIFFERENT: MAKE A CHOICE

Whenever the 'gotta have it' feeling has you reaching for your credit card, switch off the auto-pilot by asking yourself the following questions:

• What does this purchase represent to me?
• Do I really need it?

- Can I get it cheaper somewhere else, or for free?
- Would spending money on it make it harder to meet my goals?
- How would I feel if I bought it?
- How would I feel if I didn't buy it?

By asking yourself searching questions such as these you start to put your mind back onto your money. Spending with power is all about spending consciously.

Tidy up your purse

The artist, Tracey Emin, reads keys. She says she can tell a lot about a person from the number of keys they have, the number of redundant or unassigned ones, the general appearance of the key ring and so on. It sounds a bit far-fetched but, when you think about it, your appearance and how you deal with your personal belongings do reflect aspects of your character – such as whether you are tidy or sloppy, organized or all over the place.

It follows, therefore, that your attitudes to money are probably reflected in the state of your purse. If you need to improve your money-management you might start with your purse. Is it bulging with ancient, faded receipts and out of date membership and business cards, or is it a model of neat organization?

Overall, your purse is a pretty good indicator of how much you respect money. Personal finance guru Suze Orman says that people who don't respect money are less likely to keep it while those who respect it are better at handling it – and at getting it. Their finances are more likely to be well-organized – and they are more likely to be well-off. Which are you?

What's your purse-onality?

Take a look at your purse now – what does it say about you?

- **Does the style of purse reflect your attitude to money?**
  Is it smart and business-like? Funky and frivolous? Is it maybe a bit young for you (and reflects an immature attitude to money)? Or is it a designer copy because image is all-important?

- **Are the notes crisp and stored flatly, all facing the same way? Do you have them in order, lower denominations going up to larger ones?**
  Or are they just stuffed in, jumbled up with receipts, tickets and old shopping lists? How much clutter is there?

- **Do you have a small amount of change?**
  Or is it bulging with coins – perhaps because you break into a new note every time you buy something? Or have you never bothered to remove those foreign coins after last year's holiday?

- **Does it contain just one credit card and one debit card?**
  Or have you got a full set – every type of credit card and one for almost every store you've ever visited? Do you have to perform a juggling act with them whenever you pay for something?

- **Is it emergency proof?**
  Is your name and address in your purse, to increase the chances of getting it back if lost – or even in the case of a medical emergency?
  Is only essential information kept there? E.g. PIN numbers are never stored with the cards they relate to.

Wake up to where the money goes

Noticed how pay rises seem to evaporate? When your salary increases does your spending do the same? Then you're no better off – it's called salary creep. In order to have more money, you need to spend less – obvious, really. In fact, cutting back on your spending can be like getting a pay rise. Just as one teeny extra biscuit a day can add up to pounds of extra weight over a year, those trivial daily purchases would, over time, translate into a more significant cash equivalent than you might imagine.

For example, if your Starbucks habit costs five pounds a day, you'd save more than £1,000 a year if you were to buy a flask and boil the kettle. And buying bottled water?

Tap water really is safe to drink in this country. Moreover, did you know that saving £5 a day over forty years would, with the miracle that is compound interest, earn you £1 million? Feeling motivated?

DO SOMETHING DIFFERENT: LOG YOUR SPENDING

If you have a spending problem, then it's time to find out exactly how much you're spending, what you're spending it on. But, importantly, you also need to know *why* you're spending.

- Keep a daily spending diary.
- As well as recording everything you spend, note down how you're feeling and the times of day that you shop. This will help you to wake up to the habits you're subconsciously repeating and the triggers that spark off a spending binge. It will also help you to spot your wants and needs so that you become more aware of your spending habits, and less reactive.
- Take a diary or notebook everywhere with you for a week and write down absolutely everything you spend.

Track your spending

You can make your money stretch further by working out precisely where it's going. Facing up to where your money goes is often the hardest part of the process but once you've done that it just gets easier.

This is an exercise well worth doing – you don't have to have to be on the brink of financial disaster to benefit from it. If you're working toward any goals, just take a look at your cash flow and adjust what you are spending to make ways of funding them. Simple.

And adjusting your spending does not mean living on bread and water, it's about having power over what you do with your money so that it doesn't control you. It's about minding your money, rather than spending mindlessly – it does not have to be a no-fun policy.

You probably have more than a sneaky feeling about what your spending weaknesses are. Even so, it's worth getting out your bank statements, chequebook stubs and credit card bills to review the full picture – are some of those necessities really luxuries in disguise? Be honest with yourself, face up to your spending demons and try to spot exactly where all your money goes. Remember, life's a lot more fun when you know all your bills have been paid.

We've found this exercise has helped lots of our trainee Sheconomists. It's something you need to do over the long term, but we're sure you'll find it useful. Fill in the Income and Spending worksheet at the end of this chapter or download it from our website at www.sheconomics.com

See the exercise as a way of learning about yourself and to helping you get the things that really matter to you in life.

Here's our step-by-step guide to getting the most out of it. (If you have joint finances with your partner, do the exercise together.)

1. Note down your take-home pay – how much you earn *after* tax and other deductions. And add any other income that you receive, like tax credits, child benefit and rental income.
2. List all your direct debits and standing orders – mortgage, loans, insurances, utility bills etc. Get the figures from your bank statement or you can ask your bank to send you a list.
3. Record your day-to-day spending: food, petrol, drinks, taxis etc. These are costs that tend to vary from month to month.
4. Keep a spending diary. It's the easiest way to track everything you spend. It highlights your spending habits and where the money leaks are.
5. Write down any occasional spending: car repairs, holidays, gifts etc. This is the area that trips most of us up – we're doing OK then we're hit with three big expenses in one month.
6. Work out the monthly equivalent of these occasional costs (so they won't take you by surprise in the future).

Annual costs have to be divided by twelve. For the monthly equivalent of a quarterly cost, divide it by three.

Lara's story

Remember how badly out of hand Lara's spending had become? Rising debt, no hope of owning the home she longed for. And how low her self-esteem had sunk – she felt sick at herself. To her great credit Lara decided to face up to the fact that she had a problem, got to the root of it and took control of her spending.

When Lara did the Income and Spending exercise she was surprised at how much her spending on coffee and croissants added up to – just £2.80 a day amounts to well over £50 a month. But the biggest shock was her monthly clothes spend, which added up to the size of a small mortgage, and it was this that spurred her to take positive action.

Instead of reaching for her habitual shopping fix she said 'no' and started to tackle her stress by Doing Something Different. She began to break her shopping habit when she joined a dancing class two evenings a week after work. That helped her burn off negative emotions in a way that was healthier for her mind, her body and her bank balance.

Feeling energized and more motivated, Lara then committed to a cash only regime. She worked out an affordable weekly spending allowance, divided it by seven and just took that amount out with her every day.

At first, leaving her credit cards at home felt like abandoning an old friend, but for the first time Lara felt what it was like to spend with power, to exercise her own control and, with that, her self-esteem improved and her anxiety began to abate.

Tracking her spending helped Lara start spending with power.

One of our trainee Sheconomists discovered the power that tracking her spending gave her and knew she'd never want to go back to how she was before:

'I got myself into a lot of debt and knew something needed to be sorted out. I write everything down monthly: my outgoings and what I have left out of my wages – then everything I spend through the month gets taken off as I go along, so I know where I am with my money all the time. I have been tracking my spending for three years now and I wouldn't go back. I've long since stopped going shopping for something to do – I don't

_crave the buzz like I used to – and I've nearly cleared
my debt.'_

Tracking where the money goes will show up your
spending triggers: working late means a takeaway, tough
time at work means a shopping treat, anything with the
word bargain on it. Identify your triggers and break old
habits.

If you have money left when you deduct your expenditure
from your earnings then you're in the black,
congratulations. But before you throw a party to celebrate,
remember, first you need to pay off any debts – and it
would be wise to boost your savings towards the things
you really want in the future. So, ideally, immediately divert
any money you have after deductions towards debt, or
into a savings account.

Tip

_Try calculating three months' worth of spending and
taking the average. That'll give you a more realistic
idea of what you spend in a typical month. If you have
online access to your bank and credit card accounts,
have a go at downloading your statements onto a
spreadsheet and analyse your spending this way.
Or you can buy software, such as Microsoft Money, to
do the analysis for you._

The power of a spending plan

Time to think budgets, but let's see it more as a 'power spending plan'. In the money tracking exercise you saw where your money has been going. The idea of a spending plan is now to give you the power over where it goes in the future. You can use it to work out which items of spending to prioritize and the ones you want or need to cut back on. If you owe money, you'll need it to help you work out a budget for repaying the debt. And, if you're starting to wake up to the need to make your money work for you, it'll help you figure out a way to fund a pension or other savings or investment scheme.

One of our trainee Sheconomists described how she felt about her spending plan:

'I took my head out of the sand two years ago when I realized the [monthly] juggling of no disposable income and numerous credit card payments was a ridiculous place to be. I now have a set budget which I actually enjoy keeping to.'

You'll find a Monthly Spending Plan after the Income and Spending worksheet at the end of this chapter. Use it. Decide how much to allocate to each area of spending. For example, if you currently spend £400 a month on food and know you need to cut back, try reducing it to £300. Make this kind of adjustment wherever you can. You know the areas of spending you can play with.

If you can't face doing this exercise on your own (or feel you're slowly losing the will to live) ask someone to be your mentor – maybe a non-judgmental friend who's good with money and willing to help out. When you've filled in your spending plan, give yourself a great big pat on the back and put it somewhere safe so that you can refer to it easily and keep it prominent in your mind. You could also ask your mentor to meet up with you from time to time to help you stick to the plan and monitor it.

Most spending plans fail either because they're not realistic – like if you currently spend £200 a month on clothes but allow not a penny for clothes in your budget – or because nothing has been set aside for occasional expenses like annual car services, dentist's bills and holidays that come along and blow the budget. And don't underestimate the cost of the little things like snacks and newspapers, which soon add up.

Try some of the suggestions below then we'll move on to how to monitor your spending plan.

Tip

It's hard to keep track of cash spending. Keep a check on how much you withdraw in cash each month and write down where it goes. From now on, get into the habit of keeping receipts for cash purchases, particularly if you're a regular visitor to hole-in-the-wall cash machines.

Ten ways to release your inner miser

1. **Shop around for the best deals** Don't automatically renew your mortgage with your existing lender or your car and household insurances with your current insurer. And certainly don't be tempted to use one lender for all your debt. Get yourself an independent broker for your mortgage and try www.moneysupermarket.com for comparing loans and household insurances.

2. **If you owe money on credit cards** Transfer the balance to one offering an introductory rate of 0 per cent. Use any spare cash to reduce the debt, rather than waste it paying interest. Look at the best-buy tables in weekend newspapers or visit a comparison website like www.moneyfacts.co.uk to find cards offering the best deals.

3. **Slash your gas and electricity bills** Tariffs offered by different providers do vary so use an energy comparison site such as www.uswitch.com or www.switchwithwhich.co.uk

4. **Use price comparison websites** if you're after a new MP3 player, washing machine etc. Check out online offers and do a price comparison (e.g. www.kelkoo.co.uk) before shopping on the high street. Check out websites that give you the secret codes for getting money off your online shopping (e.g. www.vouchercodes.com). And you can earn money while you shop online through cash-back shopping sites such as www.greasypalm.co.uk

5. **Find the cheapest place to buy petrol** Visit www.petrolprices.com

6. **Search out the cheapest tariffs for phone calls** Visit www.18185.co.uk for cheap calls to UK numbers, as well as good international rates. And www.onecompare.com for the best mobile phone deals. Check out other tariffs at least once a year to see if you're getting the best deal. And try negotiating money off your mobile phone bill instead of upgrading your phone.

7. **Check what you're paying on each insurance policy** and in exactly what circumstances the policy would pay out. Decide whether they're worth having and if so, whether you could get any of them cheaper. Don't be hoodwinked into buying financial products that you don't need – like payment protection on your loans. Shop around for home, car and travel insurances by visiting www.moneysupermarket.com

And try www.cavendishonline.co.uk for cheap life and critical illness insurance.

8. **Have money-saving rules and stick to them** Only order tap water with a meal, don't buy takeaway coffee, steer clear of ATMs that charge for withdrawing cash, never withdraw cash from your credit card, return clothes/goods that are no good. Only use the minutes and texts allowed within your mobile phone tariff and never phone non-geographic numbers like 0845 or 0870 but use www.saynoto0870.com to find alternative numbers instead.

9. **Stop lining the gym-owner's pockets** If you don't go regularly, switch to a pay-as-you-go gym and ditch the direct debit.

10. **Become an old haggler!** Barter goods and services by joining your Local Exchange Trading Schemes (LETS). You can 'buy' goods using tokens and 'earn' tokens by providing a service back, e.g. baby-sitting or window cleaning. Check in your library for any local scheme. And try haggling in shops too – you may be pleasantly surprised. Visit www.howtohaggle.com

DO SOMETHING DIFFERENT: TRIM YOUR FOOD SHOPPING

Our appetite for luxury, gourmet food is denting our bank balances. Try one or more of these ideas for reducing your food shopping bills:

Make a list before you go shopping
Stick rigidly to it and you'll avoid impulse buys 'falling' into the basket.

Do your shopping online
Despite the delivery charge it limits how much you spend and is the best way to keep to a food budget Visit www.mysupermarket.com to compare different supermarket prices. And check out www.madaboutbargains.co.uk and www.fixtureferrets.co.uk for offers and promotions from the main supermarkets.

Buy seasonal and locally produced food
It's often cheaper and cuts down on food miles – a greener way to shop. Look out for local farmers' markets, farm shops and fruit and veg markets. If you drop by before they pack up for the day you can buy stuff for a fraction of the full price.

Avoid high-priced brand name products
Supermarket own-brand products are cheaper options. Pick up an own-brand can of tomatoes or pasta and, usually, you can't taste the difference.

Target your shopping
Don't look down on stores like Lidl: they can be great for certain goods, like tinned food, bulk loo paper, fabric conditioner and cleaning products.

Don't get sucked in by special offers
Buy one get one free is only a good deal if it's for something you'd normally buy and is non-perishable or freezable. If you just end up eating twice as much or binning one that goes past the sell-by date, it's madness.

Make use of what's in the cupboard
The food waste in this country is shameful. Four million tons of perfectly good apples get binned every day. Check out www.lovefoodhatewaste.com to see what delicious dishes you can cook up from your bread crusts and a broccoli stalk.

Monitoring your spending plan

So you've got your spending plan sorted. Now it's just a case of keeping to it. There are various ways of doing this, but one great way is to get into the habit of regularly downloading your bank statement onto a spreadsheet (ask the bank if you don't know how) and using it to keep a close eye on different areas of spending. If counting every penny feels too obsessive, then just monitor those areas of spending that you're trying to cut back on – especially any personal spending vices. For a lot of the women we spoke to they include: eating out, taxi fares, clothes and presents. Keep a spending diary to record those expenses whenever they crop up and regularly check them against your plan.

The more you do it, the more routine it will become and the more you'll enjoy being in control. If you've been plagued by out-of-control feelings in the past, this will give you a kick that many clients say feels as good as the buzz they used to get from shopping.

Here are some ideas to help you stick to the plan:

- **Pay your fixed monthly costs by direct debit** Make sure they go out just a few working days after your salary hits your account. Then you'll know that the important stuff's paid for and thus what's left for the month. And you'll only need to monitor variable and occasional costs.

- **Use cash to help you stick to a budget** Calculate an affordable weekly spending allowance for things like going out, clothes, drinks, books, CDs, etc. Then take enough cash out at the start of the week to cover those and make it last the week. No cheating though.

- **Don't be too rigid with your plan** If you need to overspend in one category, don't feel like a failure. Just try to reduce spending in another area that month.

- **Find a way of making it fun** Set yourself mini goals. Maybe save by not eating out one month and inviting friends for dinner and asking them to each bring a course.

- **Avoid using credit cards** There's nothing more disheartening than paying a bill six weeks after your shopping trip. Use a debit card instead so that you can keep a better track of spending.

- **Record everything you spend against your budget** Use a notebook or computer spreadsheet to do this. Divide it into sections for each type of expense, like food, petrol or travel expenses, and have a column for the cost and another column for what's left in your budget. Then, when you buy something, note it down in the appropriate section and work out what you've got left to spend that month.

- **Plan a way of spreading the cost of occasional expenses** For example, start a holiday savings account and put away a bit each month. The same goes for car repairs and presents. By opening a savings account with your main bank, you can transfer money quickly and easily between accounts. This way you'll have the money when you need it, rather than a big dent in your finances every few months. Don't kid yourself that these are real savings though – they're more for planned future spending – so you ideally need to build up some additional savings for emergencies.

Sometimes a day-a-week doing – or not doing –
something acts as a reminder and stops those bad habits
creeping back in.

It could look something like this:

Money-free Monday Your no-spend day
Tally-up Tuesday The day you block out thirty
minutes to tot up the figures
Walk-to-work Wednesday Leave the car at home
and walk at least part of your journey
Take-your-own-lunch Thursday Pack up a healthy
treat
Frothy-Friday The only day you indulge that
cappuccino habit

Make up a few of your own. Add monthly checks too, like
aiming to have at least two shop-free weekends a month.

Do build in plenty of feel-good, cheap and cheerful treats
that will take the place of your spends. When you're being
pulled by a strong desire to spend, try and feel a sense of
pride at having got your finances under control. If you're
denying yourself all the time it'll rebound on you, as this
trainee Sheconomist found:

*'I want to spend money when I don't have any, and
when I'm trying to be good by depriving myself and trying*

to stay within budget – that's when I seriously go mad and spend, spend, spend.'

Don't let economizing turn you into a miserable grump and be careful about getting trapped in self-limiting beliefs. So what if you've messed up in the past? Learn from previous attempts and believe that this time it'll be different. Think positively and focus on what you have, not on what you think you should have. It takes willpower but it will transform your outlook – you'll start feeling richer. The key thing is to be motivated, to stay in control and to spend with power.

Retail 'therapy' is a myth: find alternatives
In a nutshell, shopping is not the route to happiness. But what do we replace it with? When it comes to putting a spring in our step, what can top a new pair of shoes? Or a Mac lipstick for putting a smile on our face? We all need rewards and treats in our lives – we deserve them, don't we? But take a close look at what we really need and we'll see it doesn't come with a receipt. The solution to regaining real and lasting happiness is to get our highs from life, not from shopping.

More than half the women in our survey said they would spend less if they had other ways of cheering themselves up. Modern life has squeezed out those other ways and, for many women, it seems shopping is all that's left for them. To counter this we have to strip money of the power we've deluded ourselves it has as a cure-all. It's time to refocus on what really makes us happy in life.

What would you save if your house was burning down? Would you battle through the flames to grab your Gucci handbag? Researchers have asked people about their most treasured possessions. Women name photographs, love letters or memorabilia – relationships and meaningful experiences matter most to us. Women's most treasured possessions are loaded with sentiment so that, when push comes to shove, we actually don't give a damn about all that other stuff we've been so busy accumulating. For men it was cars and music – they value their possessions in a more pragmatic way.

When the going gets tough, it's a fact that the not-so-tough go shopping. More than half of the women we surveyed told us they shop when feeling low. More than a third of women suffering from depression reach for the retail equivalent of Prozac – that is, they shop in an attempt to cure themselves. Except it doesn't work.

It is a myth to think that shopping can be a cure for feeling down and escaping worries, and to refer to shopping as retail _therapy_ only keeps the myth alive. Spending does not cure depression. Indeed, it can cause depression: all the problems overspending stores up for the future can only add to the underlying problem.

The Office for National Statistics says that one in four of women's trips outside the home is for shopping. Also, according to research by GE money, UK women spend more than eight years of their lives shopping. Stop and think about that for a moment. More than eight years. That's twenty-five thousand, one hundred and eighty-four hours and fifty-three minutes, to be depressingly precise.

Mull over that eight years next time you're queuing to hand over your hard-earned cash for another object of desire that a merciless marketing person has seduced you into thinking that you can't live without. Just imagine what you could achieve with eight years of time to play with. Think what you might do that would really make you feel good: an Open University degree, perhaps, or even a doctorate, learn to play a musical instrument, run a marathon or learn to speak Mandarin.

By rediscovering – or discovering for the first time, perhaps – that you can find pleasure in the non-material you'll know what real, lasting happiness feels like. It'll do wonders for your self-confidence and it will provide positive proof to dispel the retail therapy myth. It's all about breaking your shopping habit and regaining control of your life.

Some of the alternatives to shopping that we're proposing you try here will probably surprise you and may, on the face of it, not look that exciting or appealing. Nevertheless, all the suggestions are founded on solid, psychological recipes for happiness and wellbeing. Giving away money for example. Research has shown that giving money away makes us happier than spending it. Student participants were given money and told either to spend it on themselves, or on someone else. Those who had to spend on another measured higher on happiness scales than the ones who'd indulged themselves. So, handing over £20 to a friend in need should, in theory, make you feel better than handing it to the sales assistant in Top Shop.

Life enhancing, me-nurturing things to do instead of shopping

Stay in and cook

Time spent being creative in the kitchen yields more treats and more joy than shopping. There's nothing like the smell of home cooking wafting through a warm kitchen to make you happy. Food is, after all, one of our most basic pleasures. Why spend money on an improbably coloured, overpriced ready meal when you can create something delicious in your own kitchen? Baking a cake is loads more satisfying than buying one and a humble tin of chickpeas turns into hummus at the whiz of a food processor's button and the squeeze of a lemon. And soup-making is ridiculously easy, unbelievably healthy, cheap and satisfying too.

Spend time with people you value

Our most precious moments in life come from connecting with people who matter to us, not gazing into shop windows. If you invest in family, friends, neighbours or colleagues you're less likely to experience loneliness, depression or eating and sleeping problems. Starting new friendships or rekindling old ones, walking the children to school, spending time with a neighbour or elderly relative can all make you feel good. Make the effort to join neighbourhood groups, community organizations, charities or clubs. These social support systems are vital to self-nurturing, bring long-lasting rewards and are a distraction from spending money.

Plant or grow something

Can you remember the excitement you felt as child when some seeds sprinkled onto cotton wool magically sprung up days later into mustard and cress? Recapture that sense of achievement by planting bulbs, seeds, herbs . . . anything you like. Try growing your own food: you don't need much space to grow salad leaves and herbs. A packet of rocket seeds will keep you in leaves all summer – no more expensive, meanly packed bags of leaves for you. Or, consider sharing an allotment with friends – if you can get hold of one, they're highly sought after these days. People who share their offices with indoor plants are less stressed than those whose offices are devoid of any greenery. Even caring for plants has health benefits; elderly nursing home residents who tended a pot plant lived longer than those who didn't.

Enjoy thrift

Clothes swapping, thermos carrying and packed lunches and good, old-fashioned tap water are all gaining appeal with the Sheconomist. Not only are you saving money, you'll be doing your bit for the planet, too. Walking or cycling to work is cheap and healthy and you'll arrive at the office feeling really uplifted from the buzz that exercise gives. You can still enjoy treats but search out some cheap ones: give up £50 facials, instead buy a 99p mudpack from Superdrug and feel secretly smug when no one notices a jot of difference.

Slow down when you shop. Stores hide the best bargains away and push the things they want you to buy in your face. Better still, shun supermarkets and shop locally and at farmers' markets instead.

Expand your mind

A cultural experience will excite your brain cells and keep
you contented for longer than any shopping expedition.
Cinema, theatre, a concert, the opera, a ballet, the circus
etc: go to something you've never tried before. When did
you last visit an art gallery or museum? If the last time was
in the company of your schoolteacher, go back now and
discover the (free) treasures and pleasures you've been
missing. And when did you last read a book that really
made you think? Try swapping your local for the library
one lunchtime. New passions will excite you and boost
your self-esteem.

Get outside

If your day goes something like this: home-car-train-office-
shop-office-pub-train-car-home you're probably not
exposing yourself to enough daylight. You need a burst of
sunshine to make vitamin D (also known as the sunshine
vitamin because it increases energy and has health
benefits). Take a nap in the park, soak up the winter
sunshine, sit outside a café and people-watch, feed the
ducks: however chaotic your life is, you'll feel your mood
lift and your problems shrink. Research has also shown
that a walk in the country boosts self-esteem, whereas a
walk round a shopping centre lowers it, so what better
reason to don the walking boots?

Visualize the new you

Visualization is a way of using your mind to help you achieve an aim. Put simply, it's based on the premise that if you concentrate on imagining that something is so then it will, in reality, become so.

Concentrate and imagine yourself and a group of friends sitting around chatting. The conversation turns to money and the horror stories emerge: unpaid bills, astronomical credit card debts, uncontrollable spending binges . . .

Imagine that you sit and listen to these stories sympathetically, but with a comforting sense of relief and more than a little smugness – because you sleep soundly knowing that your bills are covered and your credit cards are paid off. You know that you have the self-discipline to rein in your spending when you need to, yet you have a great quality of life, too. You reap huge joy from the non-material apects of life.
You feel strong, confident and powerful.

My Sheconomics Checklist
Law 3

How are you doing on spending with power ✓

I am my own person and can resist media/celebrity pressure	
I don't get my kicks from shopping and don't need a regular 'fix'	
If I want something I am happy to wait for it, and save if necessary	
I know my rights – asking for refunds or discounts doesn't bother me	
I don't spend more than I earn each month and I know where my money goes	
I'll Do Something Different if my spending gets out of control	

Your Sheconomics Monthly Income and Spending worksheet

Income	Monthly Equivalent
Salary paid after tax & other deductions	£
Child benefit/tax credits/state benefits	£
Maintenance payments	£
Interest/investment income	£
Rental income	£
Other	£
Total Income (1)	£
Direct Debit/Standing Orders	Monthly Equivalent
Mortgage/rent	£
Loan repayments (loans/hp)	£
Credit repayments (store/credit cards)	£
Council tax	£
Water/gas/electricity	£
House buildings/contents insurance	£
Service charge	£
Life/health insurance	£
Car insurance	£
Travel insurance	£
Pet insurance	£
Childminding/nursery/school fees	£
Landline telephone/internet/mobile phone	£
TV licence/rental/Cable or Sky TV	£
Pension contributions (if not deducted from pay)	£
Regular savings/investments	£
Other	£
	£
	£
	£
	£
Total Direct Debits/Standing Orders (2)	£

Variable Day-to-Day Costs	Monthly Equivalent
Bank charges	£
Food/household expenses/toiletries	£
Cosmetics	£
Cigarettes	£
Petrol	£
Travel expenses (including taxis)	£
Classes/pocket money for the children	£
Vet bills	£
Cleaning (car/windows/house)	£
Laundry/dry cleaning	£
Hair-/nail-care/beauty treatments/massage	£
Eating out/entertainment/drinking	£
CDs/books/magazines/newspapers	£
Hobbies/clubs/sports	£
Clothing & accessories	£
Coaching/counselling	£
Charity	£
Lunch at work/snacks	£
Unallocated cash spending	£
Other	£
	£
	£
	£
Total Variable Day-to-Day Costs (3)	£

Occasional Spending	Monthly Equivalent
Car tax/service/repairs/MOT	£
Furniture/home improvements	£
Dental/eye care	£
Child/school expenses	£
One-off goods (e.g. electrical items)	£
Trips to visit family	£
Cards/gifts (including Xmas)	£
Holidays	£
Other	£
	£

	£
	£
Total Occasional Spending (4)	£

Summarize the totals in the table below:

	Monthly Income	Monthly Spending
Total Income (1)	£	
Total Direct Debits/Standing Orders (2)		£
Total Variable Day-to-Day Costs (3)		£
Total Occasional Spending (4)		£
Totals	£	£

Disposable Income = Monthly Income minus Spending   £

Your Sheconomics
Monthly Spending Plan

Income	Monthly Equivalent
Salary paid after tax & other deductions	£
Child benefit/tax credits/state benefits	£
Maintenance payments	£
Interest/investment income	£
Rental income	£
Other	£
Total Income (1)	£

Direct Debit/Standing Orders	Monthly Equivalent
Mortgage/rent	£
Loan repayments (loans/hp)	£
Credit repayments (store/credit cards)	£
Council tax	£
Water/gas/electricity	£
House buildings/contents insurance	£
Service charge	£
Life/health insurance	£
Car insurance	£
Travel insurance	£
Pet insurance	£
Childminding/nursery/school fees	£
Landline telephone/internet/mobile phone	£
TV licence/rental/Cable or Sky TV	£
Pension contributions (if not deducted from pay)	£
Regular savings/investments	£
Other	£
	£
	£
	£
	£
Total Direct Debits/Standing Orders (2)	£

Variable Day-to-Day Costs	Monthly Equivalent
Bank charges	£
Food/household expenses/toiletries	£
Cosmetics	£
Cigarettes	£
Petrol	£
Travel expenses (including taxis)	£
Classes/pocket money for the children	£
Vet bills	£
Cleaning (car/windows/house)	£
Laundry/dry cleaning	£
Hair-/nail-care/beauty treatments/massage	£
Eating out/entertainment/drinking	£
CDs/books/magazines/newspapers	£
Hobbies/clubs/sports	£
Clothing & accessories	£
Coaching/counselling	£
Charity	£
Lunch at work/snacks	£
Unallocated cash spending	£
Other	£
	£
	£
	£
Total Variable Day-to-Day Costs (3)	**£**
Occasional Spending	**Monthly Equivalent**
Car tax/service/repairs/MOT	£
Furniture/home improvements	£
Dental/eye care	£
Child/school expenses	£
One-off goods (e.g. electrical items)	£
Trips to visit family	£
Cards/gifts (including Xmas)	£
Holidays	£
Other	£
	£

	£
	£
Total Occasional Spending (4)	£

Summarize the totals in the table below:

	Monthly Income	Monthly Spending
Total Income (1)	£	
Total Direct Debits/Standing Orders (2)		£
Total Variable Day-to-Day Costs (3)		£
Total Occasional Spending (4)		£
Totals	£	£

Disposable Income = Monthly Income minus Spending £

Chapter 5
Law 4: Have goals

'My Zen teacher also said: the only way to find true happiness is to live in the moment and not worry about the future. Of course, he died penniless and single.'

Carrie Bradshaw (actor), *Sex and the City*

Lose weight. Stop procrastinating. Fall in love. Write a book. Be happy. Get a tattoo. These are the all-time most popular entries on the website 43things.com where people post the things they most want to achieve in life. The site is also littered with literally thousands of money-related goals: make money, save money, have more money, budget my money, not worry about money.

Why do people go to the trouble of posting their goals on such websites? Because these would-be achievers can not only feel assured that they're not alone, but also gain from being egged on and supported by fellow site users. State clearly – publicly or privately – what you want in life and there's more chance it will happen: writing down or typing out your goals is a great strategy, it kick-starts the process of you taking action. The successful businessman, author and motivational coach, Robin Sieger, goes so far as to say that we attract into our lives what we think about.

That, of course, is fine if you know what you want in life – you can make it your goal, then take steps to achieve it. And let us stress, we are talking about goals here, not dreams. A dream is vague and relies on chance, or even miracles, 'I wish I could be mega-rich.' A goal is specific and realistic, 'My savings plan means I'll have £30,000 by the time I'm forty.' Goal-setters are acutely aware of the connection between how the action they take now will affect what they'll get in the future. And they act: 'Is that the bank manager? I'd like to discuss my business plan with you.' Or they're straight on to www.businesslink.gov.uk

When I (Karen) was aged eleven, the class swot used to declare with unswerving certainty and regularity that she would be a personnel manager when she grew up. I didn't even know what a personnel manager was but I was impressed. Her goal was clear: it would determine the subjects she studied and her early job choices; her path was set. Meanwhile, the rest of us were still trying to find our way to the careers office.

Goals of course vary from person to person and at different stages of life. They will only become a reality if you start planning early enough. In this chapter, we're going to help you decide where you want your life to go. Then we'll talk you through the process of how to set and achieve your Sheconomic goals. There are tips to help along the way and advice on how to stay motivated.

How did you get where you are today? Did you plan ahead or did you end up here in a random kind of fashion? Will the same be true of the rest of your life? Are you going to do nothing and simply let fate take its course? If so, you'll be more likely to regret the things you didn't do than the things you did. The fact is that most of us don't plan to fail in life, we just fail to plan. Stop and think how your life would be if you had crystal clear insight into what you wanted and how to get it. That's what we can help you do.

As far as money's concerned, most women's eyes are fixed firmly on their immediate goals: buy food for supper, put fuel in the car, pick up the dry cleaning, find a baby-sitter for the weekend, meet so-and-so for lunch. When there is no money left at the end of the month, too many women just accept it, and with no long-term financial goals, nothing can change. The fact is, no matter how small your disposable income, there's always room to make goals – including goals for creating savings and paying off debt. But you have to want to do it, set that goal and plan for it.

For those still floundering in the field of uncertainty about what we want, there's help at hand in the shape of our Sheconomic strategy. You take stock of where you are now and assess where you want to be. Then you can make a plan which will include small steps that will get you there. Don't worry if your grasp of financial matters is on the shaky side, we'll show you how. We're going to help you map out your Sheconomic journey.

As with lots of the principles in Sheconomics there's more than money for its own sake at stake here, because money is implicit in most of life's goals from buying your home, getting married or having a baby to going to university or changing careers. Then there's your physical and psychological wellbeing and sense of security – your finances impact on all of them.

Here, you are aiming to be financially prepared for the short, medium and long term. Financial fulfilment beckons . . .

By having goals you'll be able to:

- Decide what you really want to achieve in life
- Know where you're headed and why
- Create a short-, medium- and long-term financial map
- Focus on the big picture and prioritize
- Draw up a plan to make your goals become a reality

- Have something concrete to aim for to ensure your motivation won't slip

Why set goals?

To a greater or lesser extent, the majority of us are prone to the pull of instant gratification, but if we can't afford it, we shouldn't be buying it – doesn't matter if it's a chocolate biscuit, a new car or a week on the Costa Smeralda. We have to remember to look after our long-term interests and, somehow, muster up the power to say 'no'. Easier said than done. But that's when goals become your best friend.

Goals take the pain out of resisting temptation. Instead of torturing yourself over what you're missing, focus on your long-term goals. Not only does it make sense to say 'no' but you'll achieve a great, new sense of satisfaction that comes from resisting impulses when you know it's serving a higher cause.

Saying no to a ski trip, for example, sits much easier if you're giddily excited about buying your first flat and are saving like mad for the deposit. Admittedly, it's much tougher when the goal is very long term, like building up savings for retirement, for example. But if you reword 'building up a retirement fund' to the more positive 'achieving financial freedom' you're more likely to stick with it.

When I (Simonne) was a financial advisor, clients would say things like: 'I need advice on getting myself a pension' or 'I've got a bonus from work and need investment advice'. We'd complete the usual exercise of finding out all the background information. Then I'd put the paperwork to one side and start discussing their goals. What did they want to achieve and why? Only then did I really know how best to advise them.

I'm always amazed how few people ever really take the time to think about what they want in life. Yet this is crucial to the money decisions they make. Now, as a financial coach, I encourage clients to venture into this too often unexplored territory before we first meet. I ask them to complete an exercise like the one on page 137 so that they start thinking about how they might use their money to achieve what they most want in life. Then that's our starting point.

I experienced the power of having a clearly defined life goal when I set up my financial coaching business. I was passionate about why I wanted to make it happen. I knew exactly what it'd look like. Experience had convinced me there was a market. My goal was crystal clear and I came up with an inspiring mission statement – with these, I could stand up to any obstacles and setbacks that came my way at the start. I'm convinced that my unyielding commitment allowed incredible opportunities to come my way and help make it a success.

There are times in life when goals are very clear and sharp, and that's when they motivate you. As well as a passion for what you're doing you also need an unwavering conviction that it's realistically possible and that it will happen. You also need to be able to deconstruct your limiting beliefs.

Whose life is it anyway? If you don't have goals you're adrift and anyone can steer you, drag you along with them or simply submerge you in their wake. By having goals you'll be moving towards your own aims in life, and under your own steam.

Caroline's story

Caroline and I worked together for nine months. From the beginning she showed clear signs of being a top Sheconomist when it came to goal setting. Caroline was a marketing director but although she was earning well, she found that her money seemed to just disappear each month. A tendency towards erratic behaviour with money left her feeling insecure and unstable.

We explored what Caroline wanted to achieve. Her biggest life goal and top priority was to own her own flat, in six months. She needed to save a hefty deposit and wanted help to make it happen. Socializing and frivolous spending were draining her bank balance and thus she wanted to increase her sense of control and responsibility around money.

Caroline's goal was pretty ambitious so we first set a budget for her spending. This itself was a series of mini goals and Caroline committed to this plan. Keeping the goals in mind, Caroline found that the budget was easier to stick to than she'd imagined. She was galvanized into action and raring to go.

Caroline reported back to me every month, and I saw how she became more Sheconomical over time. The excitement she felt about owning a property spilled over to her handling of money. She was in charge again and the wobbly grip she'd had on her finances before was changed beyond recognition.

Caroline kept her main goal to the fore by creating a 'vision board' of what she wanted: she pinned up the details of the property she wanted to buy, dotted around pictures of the furniture she liked, stuck on her mortgage offer letter and even the balance of her growing savings. Her vision was before her, in a tangible form, whenever she put the kettle on or reached for her keys. This, Caroline said, made her feel stronger and made forgoing a few dinners out and fashion fixes bearable.

At the end of our work together she laughed that the change in her had been nothing short of amazing. Although it took Caroline nine months to complete on her flat, by committing to her goals and changing her money mindset, she made something happen that she'd never dreamed possible.

DO SOMETHING DIFFERENT: DRAW YOUR GOALS

Grab a glue stick, some cheap colouring pencils and a big sheet of paper. Now create a visual representation of your goals. Draw, scribble, sketch and stick down images. It's not about creating an artistic masterpiece.

Just freely express what you want, be creative – this will help you tap into the intuitive side of your brain. You're actually preparing your brain for when your vision becomes a reality. Making your goals perceptible (in this case by drawing them), helps to reinforce them in your consciousness.

You might discover some aspects of your goals that you hadn't considered. And where you put the emphasis might help you work out what you really want*. Of course, there's nothing to stop you making your own version of Caroline's 'vision board' too.

Have fun with it.

*When college students were asked to draw a map of their campus they enlarged areas that were important or familiar to them and underestimated the size of areas not often visited.
What looms large in your drawing – and why?

Deciding on your goals

What do you want to achieve in life? Peace and security? Escape from city life? Setting up a business? Remember that dreams are out the window. Ask yourself what's really important to you then you can work out what goals you'd need to work towards to make that vision become your reality. Make your goals specific and then adapt your behaviour and actions accordingly. For example, if your goal has always been to write best-selling fiction but you work all day and spend your nights watching telly, it's reality check time.

More realistic goals may look duller than dishwater but they work. And they inject positive energy into your life. Yes, even things like repaying debt, saving for a car or deposit for a property, planning for retirement or getting that business off the ground. And don't rule out goals such as your ideal salary a year from now, the number of days a week you plan to work, the amount of return on an investment or even the value of your business at a future date.

As we said earlier, goals and priorities change over time, just make sure you've anticipated what's to come and are prepared for the future.

Here's a decade-by-decade rundown of the types of long-, medium- and short-term goals you might think about:

Twenty something You're just getting used to having some regular money coming in. You've swapped tinned tuna for wild sea bass and are cultivating a taste for dining out and fancier shops. Having life insurance or a comfortable retirement is low on your list of wants, which are more short-term. Understandably, clearing university debt, buying a car or saving for a wedding or property are more in your sights. But here's a tip: if you can find space in your head for some longer-term thinking, you'll be streets ahead of everyone else in years to come. And you'll be absolutely chuffed with yourself for doing it because it's so much cheaper to start accumulating money when you're young – the later you start the more you have to put in. Look at this:

The cost of delay.

Imagine you can only save £25 a month. Over time this can grow into a sizeable sum. At 7 per cent interest, you'd have more than £20,000 in 25 years. But if you put off saving and only start putting aside £25 a month 10 years before you need it you'd end up with a little over £4,000. That's a huge difference for making a small effort earlier in life.

Let's imagine two friends, Jane and Angie. School friends since the age of twelve, they shared their first flat together aged twenty-one. Jane put away a bit of money every month from when she was twenty-one. At thirty she stopped to have her first child and never started saving again.

Now Angie didn't get around to starting a savings plan until she was thirty-five. But then she kept it up for the next thirty years, until she was sixty-five.

So, here's a question: If each had saved £100 a month consistently over this time – Jane for nine years, leaving the savings untouched for a further thirty-five years, and Angie for thirty years – who do you think would have the biggest pot of savings at the age of sixty-five?

Assuming that they earned 7 per cent per annum on their savings, the answer is Jane. She would end up with nearly £161,000, whereas Angie would have just under £123,000. Almost a £40,000 win for the early starter! And she put in significantly less over time.

Thirty something Your money may be channelled into buying a place of your own or climbing onto the next rung of the property ladder. You're probably striving to increase your earnings but there may still be some lurking debts to pay off. Or maybe you're funding a *Hello!* style wedding or want to retrain for a new career. If you've had children there'll be an extra drain on your income and decisions about how to make best use of child trust fund vouchers. And you'll need to protect them in case you die or get ill. On top of all this, it's time you started thinking and planning for a comfortable retirement, even if you feel you've barely grown up.

Forty something You may have managed to reach your forties without doing any serious future-thinking. But it's now becoming imperative that you dust off those long-term goals and make informed decisions. Like where the money will come from if you live to a ripe old age. The children's university fees probably aren't far off. Maybe there's an exotic holiday you've got your eye on or a new car. If you've got debt, paying that off has to take priority. And though divorce may not be part of your plans, your finances should be arranged in such a way that you won't lose out if it happens to you.

Fifty something Your long-term goals are hopefully well under way. You may have tackled some medium-term ones too, like saving to buy yourself a holiday home. Shopping has lost its appeal – you've gone from wanting everything you see to rarely seeing anything you want. If the children are off your hands, any spare cash can be directed towards your goals – hopefully you haven't let them turn into 'Kippers' (Kids in Parents' Pockets Eroding Retirement Savings). Remember they've got the whole of their working life ahead of them to fund their goals. You haven't. You're not doing yourself, or them, any favours by continuing to support them.

Retirement and beyond When you're retired your goals have really undergone a massive shift. It's now less imperative to save. If you've managed to accumulate a tidy sum you can enjoy spending the children's inheritance and still have emergency monies put aside. Things like life cover matter less now – anyway, it's ridiculously expensive at this stage of life. Your goals now are to protect your income against the impact of inflation. Or to generate the best returns on your money with the right level of risk. And it wouldn't hurt to have made provision in case much further down the line your next home is a residential one.

DO SOMETHING DIFFERENT: WORK OUT HOW MUCH IS ENOUGH

Is your goal to amass enough money not to have to work? How much would you need? To put an actual figure to it you need first to work out how much you need to live on each month. Then you have to make some assumptions about investment returns, inflation and how long you're likely to live.

But as a very rough and ready rule of thumb, apply the '25 rule'. You take that monthly figure and multiply it by 12 to make it annual, and then multiply that by 25.

So, let's say you currently need £3,000 a month after tax to live on. Turn that into an annual amount by multiplying it by 12. That's £36,000 a year. Then multiply that by 25 and you get £900,000 – a really approximate estimation of the amount you'd need to have invested to generate an annual income of £36,000 a year.

Top five Sheconomist goals

While your goals must be your own, there are some that
apply to pretty much everyone. Here are our top five goals
for Sheconomic success:

1. **Pay off non-mortgage debt** Cut right back on
   spending until you've cleared your debts. Pay off credit
   and store cards in full each month.

2. **Have a Sheconomic recovery plan** That's some
   emergency funds in case disaster strikes, like if you lost
   your job or had a big car repair bill. Then you won't go
   into debt if you're landed with an unexpected expense.

3. **Start saving for retirement early** It needn't be a
   formal pension but invest money that you could
   earmark for retirement. Don't shrink from thinking about
   retirement, start as early as you can bear to.

4. **Own your home** Buy a property to live in and aim to
   pay off any mortgage by the time you retire.

5. **Protect yourself against risks** You may need
   insurance to protect you against ill health or death. This
   depends on what your employer offers, the state of
   your emergency funds, your age and whether you've
   got any financial dependents.

Set your goals

Have a go at working out your goals. The best goals are
simple and specific. Think about what's important to you,
in the short and in the long term. Your goals should
encompass the values, hopes and desires that really fire
you up from within. Psychologists refer to this as salience
and recognize its power in all sorts of human endeavours.
Your goals need to be salient to you in order for you to
remain motivated to achieve them – don't borrow
someone's else's or let others impose theirs on you.

Here are examples of goals from some trainee
Sheconomists:

- Pay off my debt within twelve months.
- Be in control of my money.
- Get married in the near future, which I reckon will cost
  £8,000.
- Increase my earnings to £60,000 by the time I'm forty.
- Have enough savings put aside for holidays and an
  emergency fund (cats, boilers, roof).
- Live within my means.
- Pay off my mortgage by the time I'm sixty.
- Build up enough funds so that I can afford to start a
  business.
- Have three months' spending money in reserve to
  fund the transition to freelance working or self-
  employment.

- Make a will. Decide how to divvy up my estate if I were to die and nominate guardians for the kids.
- Save £10,000 so that I can afford to retrain.
- Buy a holiday home in France.
- Use my annual allowance to buy an ISA.
- Get adequately insured in case I get ill or die.
- Provide for the living costs and education (nursery & university) for my kids.
- Make our available money work for us to provide an income that will eventually cover all our costs of living.

What are your Sheconomic goals?

My goals are:

_____

_____

_____

_____

_____

Next, you need to set your goals in a time frame because that forces you to decide how long you'd be prepared to tie up the money and how flexible you need it to be.

Take a look at your list and allocate a time frame to each goal – short, medium and long term. Look at the table below and read the advice that follows to help you do this.

- **Short-term goals** Those you plan to achieve within the next five years. Like building up a reserve for emergencies, saving for a holiday or for the costs of home improvements.

- **Medium-term goals** Between five and ten years away. For example, funding children's school fees or putting money aside to take a year off work further down the line.

- **Long-term goals** Ten years away or more. This might be your nest egg for retirement or the funds to cover children's university fees.

Some savings and investment products promise a higher return, or a bonus, if you leave the money untouched for a number of years. In other words you'll be penalized for dipping into it before the term is up. Others offer higher potential returns *if* you're prepared to take the risk that the money could also go down in value. And, if you've got money in a pension plan, you can't raid any of it until you're aged fifty (or fifty-five from 2010). That's all fine if you're planning for that money to meet your medium- or long-term goal.

For short-term goals you need your funds to be more accessible so make sure you're not tying up your money in a way that's going to backfire on you. Don't put money into a five-year 'plan' when you've nothing else in reserve because if your circumstances change so that you need it, you'll forfeit interest or a bonus. Or you may, for example, be forced to cash in share-based funds at a time when markets take a turn for the worse. Unless you're absolutely certain you can leave the money untouched for the full term and get the best return, you'd be better to opt for a slightly lower interest rate and instant access.

If money is needed in the next few years (short term) savings in banks or building societies (including Cash Individual Savings Accounts or ISAs) are probably your best bet. They're easily accessible and low risk. You could opt for a fixed-term product, like bank/building society bonds or National Savings Certificates, but only on the proviso that your money isn't committed for too long.

If you can afford to tie up money for five to ten years (medium term) the investment world is open to you. There are loads of different investments to choose from including bonds, investment funds (including stocks and shares ISAs), savings plans, shares and even property. It all depends how much you're prepared to risk losing money. Usually, the more risk you're willing to take, the more chance you have of getting better returns.

If money isn't needed for ten years or more (long term), you can opt for any of the savings or investments listed above. But the difference here is that over this long-term time frame you can consider taking bigger risks because you can sit tight and wait out the bad times of the stock market. Pensions are another alternative if you don't need access to the money until you're fifty (fifty-five from 2010).

Your Sheconomic Forecast

With your list of goals and their time frames in place, have a go at inserting them into your Sheconomic Forecast (see example opposite). For now, don't worry about how you word your goals, just get them down and we'll hone them as we work through this chapter.

And don't panic. No one's expecting you to sort out the whole list right now. At this point, you're going to prioritize. Decide which goals are most important to you, the ones that really excite you and would give you the biggest buzz of all. Concentrate on those first, then identify some short and long-term goals to work on at the same time.

The importance of knowing your net worth

Before you rush off to meet your goals, you need to know where you're starting from. Knowing exactly how much money you have and how much you owe is all part of facing up to financial reality. So, we're going to start by helping you to work out your net worth.

At the same time as showing you the big picture, knowing your net worth figure helps you gauge how much you can

Sheconomic Forecast example

Short term Less than 5 years away	Medium term 5–10 years away	Long term 10 or more years away
Paying off my £4,000 credit card bill and clearing my overdraft and student loan within two years	Saving up £15,000 to cover deposit and other costs associated with buying a flat	Paying off my mortgage by the time I retire
Saving £12,000 for the cost of our wedding and honeymoon		Having enough put away so that I can have a comfortable retirement

Your Sheconomic Forecast

Short term Less than 5 years	Medium term 5 – 10 years	Long term 10 or more years

afford to put towards your goals and how close you are to meeting them. If you set goals and work towards meeting them, your net worth will almost certainly increase year by year.

Assets are what you **own**. For example, the value of your property, savings or investments.

Liabilities are what you **owe**. Such as mortgages, loans, credit cards, hire purchase agreements or overdraft.

Your **net worth** is simply the difference between your assets and your liabilities. That's what's left when you take the total of your liabilities away from the total sum of your assets.

If your liabilities add up to more than the value of your assets, your net worth is negative. If it's the other, more desirable, way around then your net worth is positive.

Work out your net worth

Don't skip this, it's important. We can't emphasize enough how crucial your net worth plan is to goal setting. It forces you to see the huge difference that short-term goals like clearing your overdraft or credit card will make – if these keep going up, your net worth is going to go down – but it also tells you to keep those all-important long-term goals on the agenda too.

Now, it's time to face Sheconomic truth and work out your net worth. Follow these five simple steps to fill in the table on pages 144–5 (or find an online version at www.sheconomics.com):

1. On the assets side, fill in the current values of any properties you own and each of your savings, pensions and investment plans.
Get the values by asking your providers. Leave out any final-salary occupational pension schemes but include all other types of pensions. Have a look at page 304 for an explanation of these different types of pension plans.

2. In the 'Other' column on the assets side, add the value of significant personal possessions such as your car, works of art or jewellery.

3. On the liabilities side, enter the current balances of outstanding debt – that's mortgages, loans, credit cards, hire purchase, overdrafts. Include monies you owe to others, e.g. friends or family.

4. Add up all the totals.

5. Subtract your total liabilities from your total assets to arrive at the figure that represents your net worth.

What's your net worth?

What I have (assets)

Savings	
Details	*What's it worth?*
	£
	£
	£
	£
	£
	£
Total	£

Pensions (no need to include final-salary pension schemes here)	
Details	*What's it worth?*
	£
	£
	£
	£
	£
	£
Total	£

What I owe (liabilities)

Credit and/or store cards	
Details	*How much owed?*
	£
	£
	£
	£
	£
	£
Total	£

Loans	
Details	*How much owed?*
	£
	£
	£
	£
	£
	£
Total	£

Property	
Details	What's it worth?
	£
	£
	£
	£
Total	£

Mortgages	
Details	How much owed?
	£
	£
	£
	£
Total	£

Investments	
Details	What's it worth?
	£
	£
	£
	£
Total	£

Overdrafts	
Details	How much owed?
	£
	£
	£
	£
Total	£

Other	
Details	What's it worth?
	£
	£
	£
	£
Total	£

Other	
Details	How much owed?
	£
	£
	£
	£
Total	£

Grand Total (a) £

Grand Total (b) £

NET WORTH: Grand Total (a) – Grand Total (b) = £ [   ]

What does your net worth figure tell you?

The bottom line is, well, it's the bottom line. It's telling you how much you are, or are not, worth. That bottom-line figure is what you're aiming to increase – by boosting the assets side and reducing the liabilities side.

The aim of the game is to increase your net worth year by year so it's a good idea to do this exercise once a year. It will also let you see how you're progressing with all your goals, though it's especially useful for taking a look at the long-term ones.

DO SOMETHING DIFFERENT: DECIDE ON YOUR FUTURE NET WORTH

Your net worth is your assets minus your liabilities. Calculate where you stand now. Then decide where you want your net worth to be in either five or ten years' time.

Draw up another net worth sheet (like the one on page 144) based on what you'd like the figures to be at that time. Recalculate the bottom line. Make that net-worth figure your goal. Put it somewhere prominent so that you look at it regularly.

Stay focused on finding ways of making the figures become a reality.

Keeping your goals on the right track

The secret to staying focused on your goals is to make them richly rewarding and relevant to your core beliefs and lifestyle values and to integrate them into your life. Now that's living . . .

Here are our over-arching tips to keep you on the right track:

1. **Focus on what you want** not what you don't want. Have a clear vision of the future. Make goals visible by writing lists, creating vision boards, drawing them – whatever works for you. Don't dwell on what you're trying to escape from; instead concentrate on planning for positive outcomes.

2. **Break the goal down** into bite-sized chunks and straightforward, manageable steps. Plan how and when you'll reach each step; set targets, deadlines and dates for review. Celebrate each achievement.

3. **Share the goal** Tell people about it, agree plans with a friend so that you are accountable to someone other than yourself. Find another trainee Sheconomist and support each other, talk about what success will look like and celebrate your triumphs together. Ask for help when you need it – a willing friend, perhaps, your partner, an independent

financial adviser (there's a list of these on www.unbiased.co.uk) or a financial coach.

4. **Challenge if there's a pull** to distract from your goal. Subconscious limiting beliefs, fears and even other people may stand in your way. Remove or work around obstacles that could hinder progress.

5. **Review** short-term goals and actions daily and keep them fresh in your mind. Make diary notes of actions to be taken. Take stock of medium- and long-term goals at least once a year.

6. **Have firm, positive expectations** You must be convinced that you're capable of reaching your goals and that they're achievable. Be realistic not idealistic.

7. **Do Something Different** All the thinking in the world won't make change happen; you need to take action. Ask yourself: 'What action can I take now to get the results I want? Do I need to change the way I do things to get a better outcome?'

DO SOMETHING DIFFERENT: TAKE A SMALL STEP

Do you have a money-related goal that you've been putting off? Starting a pension, perhaps, reassessing a long-standing endowment policy or separating joint finances you hold with a partner you're splitting from.

Sometimes tasks seem so huge that we put them off indefinitely. But, like eating an elephant, you can't do it all in one go. However, you can chop it up into small chunks and it doesn't matter which bit you bite off first, as long as you make a start. Don't wait for the right moment – there really isn't one! Start really small and start today.

Think of one small action – any action – that you can take today, and do it.

It can be something that seems pretty straightforward such as digging out the paperwork you need, doing some calculations or picking up the phone and starting that conversation you've been putting off.

Tip

If you're in a relationship you need to have common financial goals. Be sure you know exactly what your partner's financial goals are. Are they the same as yours? Do they complement yours or are you in a financial tug-of-war? Find out more about this in Chapter 7

Ruth's story

Ruth was at a crossroads in her life. She'd decided to split up from Steve, her partner of eight years, and that meant she would come into some money from the sale of their flat. Ruth wanted to shake up her life with a year abroad. Her dream had always been to travel round South America and Asia but she'd been tied to her job and to Steve. Now, she'd started to draw up an itinerary.

When I talked to her, however, it became clear she'd been looking at the atlas more than her accounts. Ruth admitted that she hadn't worked out how much she'd need to travel and that she barely knew what the state of her current finances were. She confessed she'd left Steve to deal with everything financial. Money matters scared her and she felt pretty ignorant about it all. Opening up about this was a big hurdle for her.

I helped Ruth set some short- and long-term goals. The most pressing first step was to separate her finances from Steve's. She also needed to pay off two credit cards, and track her spending carefully. Lastly, we set a goal of saving £20,000 over the next eighteen months – the amount we estimated she'd need to pay for her travels. In eighteen months' time she'd be ready to take a year off and go. Her long-term goal was to have a comfortable retirement –

something that she wanted to keep sight of amid the excitement of the trip.

We drew up a plan to meet each of these goals. Separating her finances from Steve's was simply a case of working through some clear action steps (as you'll see from her completed goals exercise on page 152). The proceeds from the sale of the flat would clear Ruth's debts and finance some of her trip. We created a budget and agreed on monthly meetings to help keep her on track.

We kept Ruth's retirement goal firmly in our sights too. It had to be weighed up against the need to save £20,000 quickly. Ruth had been paying into her company's pension scheme and having a pension was a priority for her. But she realized that, right now, saving the £20,000 could take precedence. Once we'd worked through the calculations, Ruth decided to throw all her financial power behind the goal of building up her travel funding then pay into her pension once again after she'd met her £20,000 goal. She could look forward to short-term fun and excitement without sacrificing long-term future security.

Ruth's Sheconomic strategy

Step 1 Life goals	Step 2 Financial goals	Step 3 Action	Step 4 By when	Step 5 How will you feel
To separate from Steve & fulfil my dream of going travelling on my own	My finances are independent of Steve's (short-term)	Write a new will	Within 1 mth	Relieved, free, excited
		Check if Steve is named as beneficiary on insurance plan, endowment policy, pension or the life cover I have through work. If so, change it	Immediately	
		Cancel Steve from my credit card & close our joint account	Immediately WITHIN 1 MTH	
To separate from Steve & fulfil my dream of going travelling on my own	I have £20k savings set aside to go travelling (short-term)	When sale proceeds comes through, put £3,600 into Cash ISA with Abbey; balance into savings a/c with Birmingham Midshires	When proceeds come through	Fantastic! The financial independence to make an incredible life choice
		Start saving £350 a month into Birm Midshires a/c so I'll have £5,000 within the next 14 months	Start after debt paid off. Complete 14 mths later WITHIN 18 MTHS	

Goal		Action	Timing	Feeling
To become financially free	I have confidence and control when it comes to handling my finances (short-term)	Pay £350 pm towards credit cards	From next month	Proud of myself, relieved & in control
		Pay off the £8,000 balance on my credit cards	When sale proceeds available	
		Stick to spending plan, monitor it weekly	Weekly	
		Organize my filing system!	Within 1 mth	
		Register with www.fool.co.uk to get regular emails to keep me thinking about finance stuff	Immediately	
		Cut up Barclaycard and keep Egg card just for emergencies	Immediately WITHIN 3 MTHS	
To become financially free	I have a comfortable retirement – living on £18,000 pa in today's terms (long-term)	Continue with work's pension scheme-estimate will provide me with about £4,500 pa (in today's terms) if I leave in 18 mths	Already doing	Amazing!! I Am totally in control of my future!
		Get state pension forecast	Within 1 mth	
		Pick up a pension again when I'm back from my travels – review extra funding needed to meet shortfall	2½ years BY THE AGE OF 65 (monitor yearly)	

My Sheconomic strategy

You can also download a copy from www.sheconomics.co.uk

Step 1[1] Life goals	Step 2[2] Financial goals	Step 3[3] Action	Step 4[4] By when	Step 5[5] How will you feel

1 What do you want to achieve in life?

2 Write a detailed description as if it has already been achieved, e.g. 'I have saved £1,000 by the end of the year', rather than 'I want to save £1,000 by the end of the year'. Make sure that it is positively phrased (i.e. not expressed as something you don't want), that it has a clear outcome and can be assessed

3 What specific action (including a daily action) will you take to make sure that you achieve this goal?

4 Set a realistic target date to have fully achieved this goal and each of the tasks needed to reach it

5 How will you feel once you reach your goal?

My Sheconomics Checklist
Law 4

How are you doing on having goals?   ✓

I focus on what I want – not what I don't want	
I believe I can achieve what I'm aiming for	
I'm working on my short-, medium- and long-term goals	
I know my net worth	
I have a plan to meet my goals with dates and targets	
I'm motivated to make my goals become my reality	
I'm willing to Do Something Different to meet my goals	

Chapter 6

Law 5: Look debt in the face

Could this be the most expensive bottle of shampoo in the world? Rushing from work to get ready for a night out with her girlfriends, a young woman – let's call her Rapunzel – remembered she'd run out of shampoo. She nipped into Boots and grabbed a bottle of her usual. Then it dawned on her that she'd forgotten to take any cash out that day. She had precisely 41p in her purse – £2.48 short of the money she needed.

Never mind, she had her credit card. But charging such a measly amount to her card was out of the question so she plucked a lipstick and mascara off the shelf, too. And then some moisturizer. She popped in her PIN at the checkout – £36.22 – and dashed home. The lipstick turned out to be the wrong colour. The mascara got lost down the back seat of a taxi. But at least she hit the town with her tresses clean and shining.

The following month was a tight one so Rapunzel missed making a payment on her credit card. In the year that followed she let a few more payment days slip and only managed to pay the minimum amount a few times. Finally, with interest, that dash into Boots cost her well over £100 pounds. And when years later she tried to get a mortgage, some companies wouldn't touch her because of her poor credit rating. Now _that's_ what we call a bad hair day.

Debt is no longer the dirty word it used to be. In the UK, university students are encouraged to take out loans to fund their education. The government no longer looks down on people who are in debt; it's actually handing out the loans. So times and our attitude to debt have changed. That's because not all debt is bad; indeed, when used in the right way it can give us spending power.

In terms of Sheconomy, debt falls into three categories – the good, the bad and the just plain ugly. Here, we'll show how good debt can really work _for_ you and is something to embrace and we'll reveal how to sort out the bad and avoid the ugly debt. In these days of easy credit, slipping into debt is as easy as falling off a lease-purchased log. So we're going to make sure you only take on debt you can afford and show how, just by knowing a few rules of the game, you can use debt to help you make money.

Whatever the size of your debt, if it's in the bad or ugly category it's not a nice place to be. So we'll also look at the hows and whys of getting into debt as well as – of course – the most painless ways of getting out of it.

By looking debt in the face you'll be:

- Differentiating between good and bad debt
- Feeling positive about good debt
- Facing up to what you owe and what it's costing you
- In control and able to make the right borrowing decisions
- Full of good ideas for how to make debt work for you
- Ready and able to become debt-free

How come we're all in such huge debt?

Wherever you look we're told that consumer credit has hit stratospheric levels and we're all borrowing more than we can pay back and spending more than we earn.
According to the charity Credit Action each household owes an average of £9,223 – that's not counting the mortgage, which raises the figure to a credit-crunching £57,683. And as a nation we're clocking up debt at the rate of £1 million every four minutes.

For most of us it happens like this. Our income barely covers our day-to-day needs. Our salary, if we're lucky, stretches just to the end of the month. Then an insurance bill pops through the letterbox out of the blue, or the car needs new tyres, or you fancy a second holiday and – whoosh – out comes the credit card or the bank balance is plunged into the red. And you never quite recover from it because next month . . . well, it's like we said.

Of course, it's hard to turn down what looks like free money. A letter from the credit card company tells you – yes, you – that they have your 'pre-approved' card with £5,000 credit ready and waiting. It's a sneaky sales pitch of course, pushing all your buttons with their underhand tactics, and it's easy to fall for such ploys. I (Karen) received just such a letter recently headed, ironically, 'We've got your interest in mind' (which has a touch of the nice, caring friend about it) but it's their interest – at a whopping 20.5 per cent APR – that they have in mind.

Lenders have been offering fairly 'cheap' money in recent years. For a time, banks were falling over each other to give us money, competing ferociously on the deals they were offering. One way or another we've been sucked in and we're paying the price for it now. According to a survey by moneysupermarket.com, a fifth of all UK adults are so cash-strapped they couldn't lay their hands on £100. But, it's not all bad news . . .

DO SOMETHING DIFFERENT: TAKE A FRESH VIEW

What we think we need to live on may be just a state of mind. Give the way you think about your needs a good shake-up by exposing yourself to alternative views. Then review whether you need to be in debt to support a reasonable lifestyle.

Try to talk to three people whose values differ from your own so that they will have a totally different perspective on debt.

Buddhists' principles, for example, guide them to a happy life without material possessions. So there's one approach.

Every day you probably pass a *Big Issue* seller on the street. Get chatting to someone who lives from hand to mouth, where every single penny matters.

Good debt

Good debt is credit that lets you get richer using someone else's money. We like that. Our message is that debt can be great. Think of it as someone else paying for you to earn money. Explore the suggestions here to see where you could take advantage of the upside of debt.

Mortgages People whinge about the cost of their mortgage but isn't it just great that you can get someone to lend you money to buy a house? Provided you keep up the monthly repayments and don't need to sell it in the short-term, it's bound to go up in value by the time you do come to sell it.

Compared to paying rent, where rises are at the discretion of your landlord, buying property with a mortgage can make budgeting easier. If you go for a fixed rate mortgage, for example, you know what your payments will be. And, over time, as your salary increases your mortage starts to represent a smaller chunk of it.

Twenty-five or thirty years might seem a long time to pay it off, but you'll own your home outright – hopefully by the time you retire. Equally, if you sell the property any money you make is tax-free – another reason why this debt is one we like.

Credit cards are the Jekyll and Hydes of the credit world – they have a good and a bad side. Their good side comes from the time that elapses from when you put something on the card to when you pay it off, which can be up to fifty-nine days. This short-term debt is interest free and can smooth your cash flow.

Say you have a big expense, like a car repair bill, to pay at a time when your bank balance is looking a bit sickly. Instead of going overdrawn to fund it you put it on plastic and pay off the card (without interest) when next month's salary goes in. But this is good debt only for the most highly disciplined Sheconomist. You must pay off the credit card bill in full by the due date or they'll slam interest on the whole amount.

There are other benefits of buying something on plastic, particularly expensive items (as long as you can afford them). If that treadmill-with-integral-spa you ordered arrives damaged, or Treadspa.com goes bust, you can claim against the credit card company. So it adds a layer of protection to any purchase.

Most of those pop-through-the-letterbox card offers we've mentioned really are bin fodder. However, there's one tiny exception and that is credit cards offering 0 per cent interest on balance transfers. With these, if you've got a big expense, you can put it on your credit card and then immediately transfer the balance to a 0 per cent one. But read the small print. Some charge up to 3 per cent transfer fees – so go for one that's fee-free if you can find one.

This can be a clever use of debt. Instead of dipping into your savings – which can be snuggled up earning interest somewhere else – you've got some free credit that you may not have to repay for six or twelve months. So, if you've spent £4,000 on credit, by immediately transferring it to a 0 per cent card you could earn you as much as £240 over a year by keeping your savings intact. Most 0 per cent deals only last for up to twelve months – the fee-free ones usually more like six months – so you'll need to pay the balance off within that timeframe or apply for another one.

Now we come to credit cards that pay you money: some cards reward you with up to 5 per cent back in cash. That's, for example, £100 back when you make a £2,000 purchase. But spending money just to get the cash-back isn't a good strategy because every £5 you get back has cost you £95. And you'll have to be a bit of a card-tart too – as we've just seen, most 0 per cent deals only last twelve months and then you'll need to change cards. It is tempting to use this system so that you make money whenever you spend, but I (Simonne) have coached several clients who shop this way and some struggle to stay in control of a spending plan because of the time lag between making the purchase and the payment date.

Take on debt today to earn more money in the future

Examples of this include retraining, student loans, career development loans and business start-up loans:

Retraining If you're in a dead-end job and you need more qualifications to step up in the world, then this kind of debt is right up your street.

Student loans don't have to be paid back until you're in work and earning more than £15,000 per annum. And interest is based on the rate of inflation so it's probably the cheapest kind of debt around. Clever students will have done their homework and turned their student loan into a nice little earner. If they can survive without using the money from the loan (by, er, working perhaps) they just take the money and invest it at a higher rate of interest than is charged on repayment, and then they pocket the difference. We'd give that ten out of ten.

Career development loans which help you fund up to two years of learning. You don't have to start repaying them until a month after the course ends (by which time you'll have landed that plum job and be drooling over your first huge pay packet). They thoughtfully hold back the interest charges while you're studying, too.

Business start-up loan If you decide you want to start your own business this type of loan could be the answer. Most banks will consider lending you money against a sound business plan if you've got good credit rating. There's lots of good advice too on www.everywoman.com.

What we're saying here is, go ahead and use debt to change your life for the better – but only as long as you've thought it all through and aren't just throwing in the towel after a nasty encounter with the photocopier on a Friday afternoon.

Take advantage of varying interest rates It's very clever to use the varying interest rates to your advantage. This means you borrow at low rates and invest the money at high rates. Lenders will always try to keep the balance of power tipped in their favour. In all your dealings with money, try to keep the odds stacked firmly on your side.

Take your mortgage, for example. Adding to it means you repay at relatively low rates of interest. The money you borrow can then be invested where it can earn more than the mortgage payments you're making. This is for the serious Sheconomist rather than the faint-hearted. It can pay well if you're prepared to take the risk. Say your mortgage interest rate is 6.5 per cent, and you can get returns of more than 6.5 per cent (that's after tax, mind you), you're quids in. The 'after tax' bit is critical. Because income from investments is taxable. So if you're a higher-rate taxpayer and your investment produces taxable income, it would have to generate at least 10.83 per cent a year to cover the 40 per cent tax liability. Or 8.12 per cent if you're a basic rate taxpayer.

Returns as high as 8 or 10 per cent a year aren't that easy to pin down and it's madness to release capital by remortgaging just to stick it in a savings account. If you do find investments that offer those kind of rates, they're often higher risk. But then if you're willing to stick your neck out and have a go, you could end up a lot better off.

For example, take the idea of raising money on your mortgage for a deposit on a buy-to-let house or flat. That's how lots of successful Sheconomists have built up decent property portfolios. They borrowed, say, £10,000 against their residential mortgage to put down as a deposit on their first buy-to-let. They then waited a few years for that property to rise in value and remortgaged both again. This released more money to put into property number three. And so on. Pass Go, collect two hundred pounds, and the rest is like Monopoly money.

But of course buy-to-let isn't a game. Everything's hunky dory while property prices are on the up. But there's a risk of the value of your investments falling when the housing market takes a nosedive. Don't take this kind of risk, unless you can always afford to ride out the bad times – you don't want to be forced to sell when things take a turn for the worse.

Don't be caught out: check out your credit rating

Before you apply for new credit, take a look at your credit rating. It's easy to get a credit report and a credit score by applying online. This is especially important if you've been refused credit in the past. For example, you may find that there's an error on your record that you can put right.

Companies you try to borrow money from will research you first through credit reference agencies. That way they'll know if you're a safe investment or a bit of a risk. Even if you've never been refused credit, you should make sure the information they have on you is correct: it may be out of date or inaccurate, in which case you can dispute it with the agencies. If you're not on the electoral roll it'll go against you on your credit rating.

Apply for a credit report from Experian (www.experian.co.uk) or Equifax (www.equifax.co.uk). You'll get the information that credit companies see when they check your history. At least you'll know why an application has been declined and, if appropriate, what you need to do to improve your credit rating.

A good way to check out credit deals without making a formal application is to do your own research online. Try www.moneysupermarket.com where you can compare loans and credit cards from lots of lenders using a Smart Search which estimates your credit score based on the brief information you provide. It helps you work out who's likely to lend to you without leaving a 'footprint' on your credit file in the way that repeated applications for credit reports do.

One of our trainee Sheconomists checked her Experian report after being rejected for credit. Why was she a poor credit risk? She was one £2 payment behind on her loan account. She'd paid back the balance on this account several months earlier, but it turned out that there was still £2 of interest remaining. This £2 debt was the only black mark against her yet it made her a bad risk. As soon as she realized this, she paid back the two pounds. Then she added a Notice of Correction to her credit file to explain the situation to future potential lenders. She also closed credit accounts that she no longer used. This had the effect of reducing her total available credit, which further improved her score.

Bad debt

Debt is bad whenever it involves paying out more money than you get back. Paying interest on a bad debt is a bit like flushing £10 notes down the loo. Yet sometimes bad debt is an inescapable part of life. We're mainly talking about consumer debt here – and by 'consumer' we mean non-essential purchases that don't have the potential to make you any money. With every will in the world, you may feel like there's no other alternative but – and you really do have to face up to this – these are the baddies to avoid:

Authorized overdrafts These aren't as squeaky clean as they sound. Many accounts offer a fee-free buffer (usually between £50 and £500) or special terms for the first year

of opening an account. While using the fee-free bit is OK –
although you've still got to pay it back so use it carefully –
going above that counts as bad debt.

But, we hear you say, 'Everyone uses their overdraft, don't
they? How else am I supposed to manage my cash flow?'
Not a good money-belief. Best to steer clear of authorized
overdrafts whenever you can. The interest they charge,
once you get past the fee-free bit, isn't usually a whole lot
different to credit card interest. This can land you with a
big owe when you already have an overstretched budget.

Buying assets that are really liabilities and going into
debt for them, is madness. That car, computer, state-of-
the-art TV is going down in price all the while you're
making your repayments. Hire purchase compounds the
poor Sheconomic sense because you don't even own the
'thing' until you've made all the repayments. This means
you don't even have the option of selling it to repay the
debt.

Using high interest credit cards to pay for anything from
a holiday, to presents for people, to a wedding even, is
bad debt unless you pay off the full balance when the bill
arrives.

Why you'll pay more when paying by credit card

Using a credit card doesn't feel like spending real money, does it? It has an unreal, ethereal quality that can lure us into overspending.

When you hand over cash, that's it gone; hand over your card and it comes back to you – and it looks exactly the same. This lack of any apparent difference fools you into believing nothing's changed.

An experiment in the US, run by Professor Drazen Prelec, demonstrated this. College students were allowed to bid in a silent auction for tickets to a popular basketball game. One group were told they could only pay by cash, the other group only by credit card. The credit card bidders bid, on average, more than twice as much as the cash buyers. Professor Prelec concluded that, 'The psychological cost of spending a dollar on a credit card is only fifty cents.' So you could say a pound spent on a credit card is a bit like spending fifty pence in cash.

Perhaps by leaving our cards at home and using cash we'd halve our spending?

Are you seeing interest payments on your credit card swallowing up your salary? Don't be afraid to shop around or swap lenders. Interest rates vary all the time – cuts or hikes in interest rates seem to make the headlines daily – and there is also huge variation between the rates different lenders charge to give you credit. A one per cent difference may not sound like much but with compound interest it can save you a small fortune.

Compare the rates of interest you're paying on your cards and loans with those offered by other lenders. Look through the money pages in the weekend newspapers and check out websites like www.moneysupermarket.com or http://www.moneyfacts.co.uk Shopping around and switching lenders requires a bit of effort but think of it as money earned. If it takes two hours of your time but you've saved £200 a year in interest, then surely it will have been worth your while.

Loans and cards taken out with the bank you hold an account with are often the easiest to arrange but they don't necessarily offer the best rates. After all, they've got your business already so they don't need to lure you in. The easiest option is almost always more expensive. But remember who's the customer here.

If your bank's overdraft charges or your credit card interest rates are crippling it's worth a cheeky call to tell them you've found a better rate elsewhere. They might – and they probably can– match the rate because they want to keep your business. If not, you've only lost the cost of a phone call because you'll switch anyway. When one of our trainee Sheconomists got her bank to agree to reduce the interest on her credit card she told us:

'I can't believe how easy it was to get my bank to agree to reduce the rate. Financial institutions have always scared me in the past. Not any more. This was liberating!'

If you have a good credit rating you can transfer credit card debt to one that charges 0%. This way, any money you repay pays off the debt rather than being swallowed up in interest. Check out the 0% balance transfer offers and ideally try to find one with no transfer fee. Look out for offers on money-saving expert Martin Lewis's site www.moneysavingexpert.com

If you've got more than one card, you can potentially sweep all your cards onto one new 0% one. Then you'll have just one payment to make every month. But if you have a poor credit rating these card issuers may either not look at you or want to charge a higher interest rate.

If you haven't a hope in hell of paying off the credit card debt within the interest-free period, look at a low-rate lifetime deal instead. This freezes the interest rate at a low APR (usually a little lower than the best loan rates) for as long as it takes you to clear the balance you've transferred. If you go down this route, don't use the same card for new purchases and treat it like a loan or you could be paying the debt for years. Remember: only making minimum payments means that debt will be lingering around you like a bad smell for years to come.

If you found GCSE arithmetic unfathomable and are worried about how to calculate how long it will take you to repay a debt at a particular rate of interest, there are lots of online calculators that'll do it for you. Just tap in the amount owed, the interest rate and repayment figure and it will tell you how long it'll take to become debt free, or how much you need to pay to get the card paid off by a certain date. Here's one to try:
http://www.whatsthecost.com/creditCard.aspx
Don't you just love the Internet?

An interest-only mortgage might be the only way you can get a foot on the property ladder. But if you do it long term without an investment plan running alongside to repay the balance, it's bad debt. That's because it never pays off any of the capital so what you owe won't diminish with time. OK, if you've found that perfect Georgian mews house for a knockdown price then an interest-only mortgage might be the way to go, but only if you're sure you can sell it for more, then perhaps downgrade at a later stage and use the equity as a tidy sum towards your next property.

Remortgaging to pay off debt This can feel like good debt, because the payments are affordable and they spread so far into the distant future they seem unreal. But remortgaging is incredibly expensive in the long run. And by taking some of the capital out of your home you're devaluing your biggest asset. Plus you may be putting your home at risk if you can't keep up repayments. (We tell you about the sometimes upside on page 165.)

Going into debt to pay off debts Taking out a high-interest loan to pay off credit cards and overdrafts is debt madness. Even switching to a lower rate card is dangerous, unless you're certain you won't take out any further debt until that's paid off. A lot of debt advisers warn against borrowing to pay off debt because people commonly build it back up again a few years later. Remember that a loan doesn't shrink the existing debt, it just moves it around – the financial equivalent of rearranging the deck chairs on the *Titanic*.

Psychologically harmful debt This is where the emotional cost to you is disproportionately higher than the actual size of the debt. Debts causing bad feeling in this category include borrowing from friends or family, borrowing to feed an addiction (see our Am I Addicted? questionnaire on page 83), borrowing to make yourself feel or look better. Change your view, deal with your emotions, read the rest of this book. Do whatever it takes. But don't shift your negative emotional balance into your bank account.

Ugly Debt

TIP

Come to grips with the notion of compounding and you'll never fall foul of ugly debt. Compounding is how the lenders make money out of lending, it's also how the rich get rich.

The Miracle and Misery of Compounding

'The most powerful force in the universe is compound interest.'

Albert Einstein

Compound interest sounds like a very, very boring phrase, yes? But it's really quite miraculous – when it's working *for* you. On the other hand, when it's working against you it's the dreary downside of debt. So it's worth sticking with this one and trying to understand how it works.

Here's a quick teaser:

If you put a penny into a jar on the first of January, and then doubled the amount you put in every day for a month (2p on the 2nd, 4p on the 3rd, 8p on the 4th etc.), how much would you have at the end of the month?

a) 62p
b) £12.80
c) £10,737,418.00

The correct answer is (c). Yes, more than ten million pounds. On the 30th of the month the amount would be more than £5 million and, of course, that would double on the 31st.

It's an extreme example (who's got a jar *that* big?) but . . .

Think about it in terms of a loan. The amount loaned attracts interest, then interest is charged on the original amount plus the interest, and then interest is charged on that, and so on. The longer that continues, the more you're paying back. The difference between day 30 and day 31 in the example above illustrates the massive difference an extra year might make to a loan period.

So think about it, too, when choosing repayment terms: the longer a loan is taken out for, the more the interest-upon-interest amount racks up. When borrowing, always go for the lowest interest rate and shortest repayment period.

When saving, compound interest works for you and the effects are quite remarkable if you start early.

Financial planner Malcolm Cuthbert worked out that if thirty-five-year-olds put the £1.80 a day they spent on a cup of coffee into their pension pots instead, at the age of sixty-five – with compound interest – they'd get £3,843 more *every year* for the *rest of their lives*.

Making only the minimum repayment on credit- or store-card debt They've got a bit of a cheek calling these repayments – you're hardly paying anything back. Interest is being added to the outstanding balance (which includes the accumulating previous months' interest) every month. It can take up to forty years to pay off a credit card by minimum payments only.

Credit card companies usually require a minimum payment of 2 per cent of the outstanding balance each month or £5 – whichever is greater. It seems so little to ask. You can almost hear them rubbing their hands. They know they'll be making money out of you for decades to come.

If you can't clear the whole balance, paying even just £10 a month more will make a huge difference. This principle of overpaying (intensifying your payments) doesn't just apply to credit or store cards, it can also make a big difference to loans. Next time you get a bonus or salary rise redirect it towards paying off your debts. You won't feel any worse off because your salary will be the same as it was before. But your debt will be reduced and that means a far happier you in the long term.

Some lenders are so enjoying profiting from your extended loan periods they'd rather you didn't spoil it for them, thank you very much – so they try to penalize you for being sensible enough to overpay. Check that your lender won't charge a penalty if you overpay and check whether they recalculate the interest as soon as the overpayment is made. If not, transfer the money you would have used to overpay into a savings account to earn interest then overpay the loan when you're outside of any penalty payment and at a time when they'll readjust your future interest payments.

Missing the payment date on your credit or store cards This is when the card companies get really ugly with you. Not only do you get fined, yes fined! You also get a black mark on your credit rating. That means trouble next time you apply for credit anywhere. Set up a direct debit, ideally to pay off the whole amount each month. Even arranging for them to collect the measly minimum payment is better than nothing.

Using your credit card to withdraw cash or writing one of those 'credit card cheques' that some card issuers provide. In this case you haven't even got fifty-odd days to pay it off. Interest starts going on as soon as you make the cash withdrawal. And at a higher rate than for purchases. Then, to add insult to injury, there's a fee charged too, up to 3 per cent. How ugly is that?

Using your credit card abroad to withdraw cash On top of all the nasties above, they slap on a currency conversion fee, too. Travellers cheques are a better bet if you're heading out of the country. Or, if you don't mind walking around with cash, pop along to a UK post office before you leave to exchange currency for free.

Using a store card Unless you can pay off the whole amount say NO. The interest rate on store cards is even more hideous than credit cards. No wonder they try to tempt you with 10 per cent off the first purchase. Play them at their own game if you like: take the 10 per cent discount then cut up the card as soon as you get home. And as soon as the bill comes, pay it *all* off.

Funding day-to-day living with credit Are you putting stuff like takeaways, drinks, taxis and magazines on your card? Afraid we're talking poor money management here. Or a desperate situation that needs sorting out quick.

Using credit to pay for household costs or other debt such as your mortgage, rent, credit cards or loans. This is an expensive solution, and a risky one, too. If things are that desperate, talk to your creditors and explain your situation to them.

Unauthorized overdrafts If you can't avoid pitching into the red, at least get an overdraft approved with your bank first. Otherwise you'll get stung with a fee (each time you go overdrawn) on top of massive interest charges.

Securing a loan against your home This is when you borrow money but sign away your own home in the event of non-repayment. Watch the conditions of loans. Unsecured loans are a far better option.

Double-digit interest rates on any loan, mortgage, credit or store card Shop around for the best deals – in the current market, you should always aim for well below 10 per cent. If lenders only offer you high rates because of your poor credit rating, this is a very loud message that you shouldn't be taking on any new debt.

Using a debt consolidation company that pays off all your unmanageable debts and 'consolidates' them into one big one, then charges you for the privilege. Instead, use one of the free impartial credit agencies (e.g. www.cccs.co.uk) or negotiate direct with your creditors (see page 203). Don't be seduced by those TV ads offering to consolidate your debts – how do you think they afford peak-time advertising slots?

Getting into debt

The I-got-dumped debt

Frankie's story

Frankie told us how her debts came about:

'When Dominic told me it was all over I shot into town and had a credit card blow out. I'm talking Prada and Gucci here, and not just one bag but four, and the shoes in just about every colour they had. I was off my head and didn't care. I think on that occasion I blew well over three thousand pounds.

'When I look back I realize I've reacted to every relationship break-up by spending money I haven't got. I suppose I think, "So what if I can't have you, I can have whatever else I like!"

'I end up hating most of the stuff because it reminds me of miserable times and I'm still trying to pay off the eighteen thousand pounds I owe on my cards.'

I needed to take emotional control. The message here, which we discussed in Chapter 2, is: deal with your emotions, don't spend them.

Lots of women – intelligent, professional women – tell us they can link their periods of highest debt to an emotional crisis. You could call it the high cost of the ''Ex' and the city'. They describe times when they're already overdrawn, or have spent the next three months' salary with one swipe of a card, yet they carry on spending even though it's madness: the voice in their head is saying: 'In for a penny, in for a pound, OK, make that a few hundred.'

Some women, when their heart has been broken, set out to mend it by spending on luxuries they hope to find comfort in. But that, as we've discussed, is no justification, nor does it justify the huge emotional and financial price they pay in the long term. Frequently, though, women's debt is the result of a plain and simple failure to delay gratification: remember that present, I-want-it-now self that we met in Chapter 4? Millions of pounds of debt are owed by people who gave in to that impulse, people who couldn't tell themselves, 'No'. *Sex and the City*'s Carrie Bradshaw was right when she said: 'Isn't delayed gratification the definition of maturity?'

Scary stuff. But let's not dwell on how we get into debt. We want to look at how the hell we're going to get out of it.

Getting out of debt

Of all the money worries that keep people awake at night, owing a lot of money is the biggest and most common. As well as the nightmare of knowing you're broke, debt is embarrassing and humiliating. And it's a problem that won't go away – in fact, it gets bigger and bigger – unless you do something about it, so the dive-under-the-duvet approach is a big no-no. The only sensible way forward is to look debt in the face. This would-be Sheconomist's story is an all too familiar one:

'I've had a problem with money since I was eighteen. At one point I had five gold credit cards. I finally saw sense and got the debt consolidated and then I realized things were spiralling out of control again – I'd spend on the credit cards after I moved the balances. I eventually cut all of them up in one go, not realizing that my spending had amounted to debt of seventeen thousand pounds.

'Currently I'm twelve thousand three hundred pounds in debt, paying back two hundred and eighty-one pounds a month over the next four years. This debt was shoes, handbags, holidays, nights out. I don't regret it in a way, I never lost sight of those memories. But apart from memories I have nothing to show for it.'

Five steps to clear debt

Here's our five-step Sheconomic solution to getting out of debt. Follow the steps and you will start to make a dent in what has seemed like an insurmountable problem. Plus, sorry to bang on about this, but we can't over-emphasize the need to start immediately. Dilly-dallying over debt will just cost you more because the interest is compounding all the time you procrastinate. That's exactly what the lenders want so they can make more money out of you in the end.

To make the process easier, we've designed a Sheconomics debt-payment plan table (find it on page 214 or online at www.sheconomics.com) which provides you with a ready-made format to use in conjunction with the steps below.

If you do nothing else, take these five steps and start looking debt in the face right now:

1. List all your debts

Make a list of everyone you owe money to, and how much you owe each one. For any cards and loans, note the minimum payments due and the interest rate being charged (the APR) for each one on the list. Then reorder the list, putting the one with the highest APR at the top, the next highest below that, and so on. Next – brace yourself – you're going to add up the total amount you owe and the total payments due. That includes at least the minimum payments on all cards.

2. Decide on priorities

Identify any priority debts. That's your mortgage, secured loans, rent, council tax, utility bills, tax, national insurance, maintenance orders or court fines. These have to be dealt with first, they're more important than other forms of debt, like credit or store cards, overdrafts and unsecured loans.

3. Pay off whatever you can

Use any savings or investments to repay or reduce any of your debt. Having savings earning 5 per cent interest is ludicrous if you have debts costing you 16 per cent interest.

4. Work out a monthly repayment amount

Decide how much a month you can put towards your remaining debts. Use our Sheconomic Monthly Spending Plan on page 118 to help work this out. Figure out ways of cutting back on spending to maximize this monthly figure. For example, could you temporarily stop regular payments into any savings or investment policy to give you more money to throw at your debt? Although check first that you won't suffer any penalties.

If you're using our Sheconomic debt-free exercise table, enter this figure in the total box under the heading 'What you plan to pay each month'.

5. Make a debt-payment plan

Work out how to split the total monthly amount you can afford to repay between your creditors. Look back at the list of all your debts that you made at Step 1. Aim to pay as much as possible towards the debt with the highest interest rate first. Keep making minimum payments on any others. Once you've paid the highest off, plough as much as you can towards the next highest. And so on until all the debt's repaid.

And, of course, set a goal of the date you plan to be debt-free and work out how much you'd need to pay your creditors each month to make it happen. Keep that debt-free day in mind to give you added motivation. Love that feeling of squaring up to debt, and tackling it.

DO SOMETHING DIFFERENT: SHARE YOUR DEBT-PAYMENT PLAN

You've made your plan and you're ditching your debt. It's vital that you stay on track.

Now think of three people who are supportive and important to you. Tell each of them about your plan. Give as much or as little detail as you like, but make sure you voice your intention.

When you make your intentions public you're less likely to default on them. And the support you'll have from people who care about you will remind you you're doing the right thing and add to the positive emotions that you're going to feel.

By following your debt-payment plan you'll be systematically paying off your debts one by one. This is our preferred option because it means you don't have to take out any further debt to pay it off.

Some women say they prefer to get rid of all the small debts first because they feel less weighed down by reducing the number of people they owe money to. So they still go through the five steps to make a plan, but their top priority is to pay off all their small debts. That's fine by us, too, if it works better for you and, most importantly, if it motivates you to stick to your debt-payment plan. But do act on the bigger debts – they'll be costing you more in interest.

If you're left with any debts where you can't even manage minimum payments, then contact your creditors straight away and try to negotiate a way forward (see Negotiate with your creditors on page 203). Whatever you do, don't ignore them, however ugly: this is all about looking debt in the face. As the writer and broadcaster Vivienne Parry says, and who can disagree?: 'Debt is a modern fact of life but to avoid our health being damaged we need to be open and honest about it . . . [this] will ensure that we get help early and avoid those two fatal mistakes, hoping it will go away and getting into more debt to solve it.'

The five-step solution works equally well if you don't have a regular income and prefer a more flexible approach. You just need to go through the steps more frequently. For example, you could complete our debt-payment plan table once a month to help you work out how much to pay each creditor that month.

Donna's story

Donna's story is typical. When she first sought my help she owed £5,800 on credit cards. Not a huge amount compared to some. But when I asked how far back this went she confessed she was still paying for stuff that she and her partner had bought together – and they'd split up over five years ago.

Donna had also missed a few payments recently. In the course of two months she'd changed jobs, moved house and been in hospital so she'd taken her eye off the money ball for a while. In addition, for the best part of the past five years, the most she'd managed on her credit card bills was the minimum payments, so the balance on the cards had gradually grown. Donna had no idea that she'd really paid back very little.

Most of her monthly payments were just paying interest. On some cards the minimum monthly payment doesn't even cover the interest so the debt itself never gets repaid. In Donna's case, the last monthly payment she made was £116, but that took only £37 off the debt – the remaining £79 was funding the interest.

By making minimum monthly payments of 2 per cent of the balance, at an interest rate of 17 per cent, it would take more than forty-nine years for Donna to pay off her debt. That's not the only shocker – she would end up paying £12,798 on top, in interest.

If Donna paid back just a little more than the minimum payment each month it would make a staggering difference. Another £10 each month would reduce the time to pay off the debt to just over twenty years, and it would save £5,305 in interest. Stretching a little further to pay an extra £25 a month (the monthly cost of her Sky subscription) would clear the debt in just over eleven years, saving £7,889 in interest. But that's eleven long years of debt.

Donna was horrified. Those numbers spurred her to make some drastic cutbacks. The goal we set was to get rid of the balance in eighteen months, without taking on any new debt. The missed payments had damaged Donna's credit rating so she wouldn't get credit anywhere else.

She would need to make steady payments of £367 a month for eighteen months to clear the card. It did mean her making a few sacrifices, including having a holiday at home this year. But Donna agreed it was well worth it to get debt-free in eighteen months instead of forty-nine years.

Donna did the right thing when she realized she wasn't getting anywhere with her credit card debt. She faced up to her problem and sought help. When it comes to owing money, different people respond in different ways. Here are a few we've come across. See if you identify with any of these . . .

The panicker

When a debt threatens to sink her, Pauline just borrows more money to pay it off. Panickers have a reactive borrow-from-Peter-to-pay-Paul approach to debt and never get around to sorting it out properly.

The mourner

Maureen refuses to see that she's responsible for her debt. It's always someone else's fault. She blames her sister for getting married and 'causing' Maureen to spend hundreds of pounds on outfits for herself and her family. When in debt mourners get resentful and lash out at others.

The unethical

Fran, on the other hand, is trying to abuse the system. She lied about a forthcoming inheritance to persuade her bank manager to give her another loan. The unethical debtor will try to avoid paying anyone if they can get away with it.

The rational Sheconomist

Rachel owes money but she's sorted her debts into order of importance. And she's negotiated repayments based on what she can realistically afford. Rational Sheconomists are the more sensible debtors; they don't run away from debt.

The rational Sheconomist looks debt in the face, takes responsibility for the situation and for sorting it out. Women, like Maureen, who are in denial often entertain unrealistic rescue fantasies, believing someone, somewhere will sort out their problems for them.

Self-responsibility is the key here. It's a principle that will serve you well in every facet of your life and, here, it means knowing that you are responsible for your debt. You got into debt and you're going to have to pay to get out of it; there's no other way around it. But you can enlist someone else to help you find the best way of doing that (see the list of agencies you can go to for free help and advice on page 204).

Tina's story

Tina had become totally disconnected from the value of money. She'd financed her lifestyle on credit for as long as she could remember. She owed £36,000 on seven credit cards and a loan. She came into my office, sheepishly, after a lunch with friends at the Ivy, and admitted she knew she was living on borrowed time – and money.

I'd asked Tina to bring along details of all her finances. She'd quickly totted up what she owed and realized she had a Michelin Man-sized spending habit.

'This was a such a painful process,' she said, 'but I'm so glad I've done it at last.' We worked through the debt-payment plan exercise and noted down the interest rate being charged by each of her creditors. The rate on the bank loan was relatively low but on the credit cards the rates were extortionately high. The minimum payments on those were costing Tina £1,030 a month.

For starters, we had to prioritize the actions Tina could take to pay off more on these cards. She could cut back on some of her outgoings to manage this. We put an Equity ISA and a pension plan temporarily on hold. We found that Tina's house contents insurance also covered her for travel, so she cancelled an unnecessary annual travel insurance policy. With those savings, and fewer restaurant meals, Tina could pay

£2,000 each month off her debt. Even at a high interest rate of 17 per cent APR, she could be debt free in twenty-one months. And if we could shave something off that interest rate, it would take even less time.

Tina ruled out moving to lower rate cards or consolidating into a loan because of her poor credit rating. She hadn't actually tested this, but she was simply terrified of checking her credit rating in case it threw up more horrors. When she did finally check, her credit report was flawless and her credit score was a very respectable 999. Even so, Tina would only have been able to transfer a proportion of her debt. Also, quite sensibly, she didn't want to make it too easy to build up credit again. In the past she'd taken on debt to pay off what she owed but had simply got into debt again. A case of having her cake and eating it.

Tina knew she had to wean herself off cards and start using cash for day-to-day expenses. And instead of getting a new card to juggle existing debt, she would ask her existing lenders to agree to reduce their interest charges. Tina was anxious initially – she avoided financial institutions like the plague. But having faced checking her credit rating she now saw that she could be in the driving seat.

Tina negotiated with four of her creditors to reduce their rates significantly. Then she transferred the remaining balance to a card with a low lifetime rate. Within nineteen months the debt was paid.

'I feel so much lighter now,' she laughed at our last session. 'Now my debt's cleared I have two thousand pounds extra monthly income. Money seems more real since I've been using cash, I don't hand it over half as easily. I've gained pounds in money and I've lost twenty pounds in weight from not eating out as often, so that can't be bad.'

DO SOMETHING DIFFERENT: NEGOTIATE A DISCOUNT

Identify one regular purchase and see if you can get it cheaper.

What do you always need to buy? Petrol, electricity, mobile phone time, insurance, dog food? Try to negotiate a discount direct with a supplier.

Or shop around and see where you can buy cheapest – from petrol prices to insurance premiums our Ten ways to release your inner miser list on page 98 tells where to go to compare prices.

Ten tips for dealing with debt Sheconomically

1. **Share the problem** If you're worried about debt talk to someone you trust or find a debt-free buddy for support. Don't suffer in silence. Opening up is a way to face your debt.

2. **Give those credit and store cards the snip** Make repaying your debt a priority. Cut them up if you can't trust yourself!

3. **Have a plan to pay back the money you owe** Make it a goal to be solvent by a specific date and use

our five-step debt-payment plan to help you get there (see page 184).

4. Apply for a credit report and credit score from one of the two main agencies in the UK: Experian (www.experian.co.uk) and Equifax (www.equifax.co.uk) so that you can check your record in case you need to shop around for more credit.

5. Steer clear of store cards They charge outrageously high interest. If you're enticed by the 10 per cent off your first transaction, take advantage of the offer. Then pay the bill in full and on time and cut up the card.

6. If you have a repayment mortgage and you're struggling with other debt, it may be worth asking your lender to consider switching your mortgage to interest-only for a short period of time. This will reduce the monthly payments until you're back on your feet. Then you can restart the regular repayments again.

7. Double or treble the price tag if you're buying something that you plan to put on your credit card and pay back through minimum payments. Because that's what it's going to end up costing you by the time you've paid for it. If it's in the sale, question whether it's such a bargain after all.

8. Know what it's costing you when you borrow money What's the interest rate and for how long? How much will you pay back in total? What happens when you're outside of any special introductory rate? Can you get a better deal elsewhere?

9. Refuse the payment protection plan Often sold as insurance to cover your monthly payments if you have an accident or become sick or unemployed, this is added to the loan, with interest, and can add thousands of pounds to the cost of the loan.

10. Avoid hire purchase (HP) It's expensive and you don't actually own the item until you've made all the repayments. So if you're using HP to pay for a car for example, it's not yours to sell until you've paid for it in full.

A loan to consolidate your debt: avoid the pitfalls

'I was getting bills, statements and reminders on an almost daily basis and I felt really stressed about it. Half the time I was letting them pile up because I couldn't face opening them. Then the sight of the pile made me feel sick. In the end a friend who works in finance told me to get a personal loan. I got a much lower interest rate than credit cards charge. I paid everything off with the loan.

*That means now I pay the loan once a month and I don't
dread seeing the postman coming up the path so much
these days.'*

This trainee Sheconomist found she could pay off her
debts with a personal loan at a low interest rate and, yes,
it can be a good way of getting a lot of creditors off your
back. But don't be lulled into a false sense of security by
thinking your debts have gone.

Avoid the un-Sheconomical pitfall that we've seen lots of
women fall into. They take out a loan or even remortgage
to repay their debts. They temporarily feel sorted so they
continue spending and then get into debt again within a
pretty short space of time. The bills mount up *and* there's
a loan to pay off into the bargain. Disaster.

As we have suggested, get the scissors out and cut up
all your credit cards (apart from one maybe for
emergencies) then cancel them by phone, and then also
in writing. That will show up on your credit record as you
having access to less available credit, which will improve
your credit score. Avoid loans that offer you more money
than you can afford to pay back, or more than you need.
And think twice about taking out loans that are secured
against your home – your home could be repossessed if
you don't keep up the payments. Shop around to see if
you can arrange an unsecured loan instead. Visit

www.moneysupermarket.com or www.moneyfacts.co.uk to compare different loans.

Taking charge of your debt in this way also forces you to get a grip on your spending habits and will help you come to terms with your emotional relationship with money and self-limiting beliefs. Once again, it's all about looking debt in the face and planning your way out of it.

DO SOMETHING DIFFERENT: FEEL THE DIFFERENCE

Many people we speak to see debt as something unavoidable; part of our day to day existence. For them it has almost become a way of life.

Take a pen and write down a Debt-Free Me description. What would your debt-free life look like? What emotions would you feel: freedom, joy, peace, independence, control?

Make a list of those feelings and see how it lifts your spirits. Decide today that a debt-free life is one worth aiming for.

Add debt to your mortgage

An easy way to borrow money either to clear debts or for other expenditure is to remortgage your property. But don't be fooled. It seems like the most affordable option, because the monthly payments will be lower. But it's probably the most expensive way to borrow money in the long term. This is because the remaining term of your mortgage – twenty years, say – is likely to be much longer than the term of any loan. So the interest is compounding year upon year and the total amount you pay back could be as much as five times what you borrowed. And, of course, it puts your home at risk if you don't keep up the repayments.

If you've got an interest-only mortgage, this will make the payments seem even cheaper. But don't kid yourself that you've found a solution to pay it off. You're just deferring the problem. It might get you out of an immediate sticky situation but as a long-term solution it's not Sheconomical.

Be mortgage-savvy

For some, an interest-only mortgage is the only way to get on the property ladder. But, as soon as you can, switch to a repayment mortgage. Or set up an investment plan to periodically pay off the debt. Many mortgages offer you flexibility to make an occasional lump-sum payment to reduce your mortgage loan. This could be an option if you earn an annual bonus, say. Or you may choose to split the mortgage into two parts – interest-only and repayment. This way at least you'll know the repayment part of the mortgage will be paid off after a set term.

Two couples, Bhavita and Mati, and Chris and Alex, were each seeking mortgages of £150,000. The repayment mortgage cost £1,012 a month, the interest-only one £812 a month.

Chris and Alex chose the interest-only mortgage – they wanted to have more money to spend on themselves each month. Bhavita and Mati went for the repayment mortgage. To help with the cost they took in a lodger who paid them £300 a month. After a year the lodger moved on. The payments were a struggle at first but then Bhavita got promoted and it soon became manageable.

Fast-forward twenty-five years. Chris and Alex still owe £150,000 because their interest-only mortgage – obviously – only paid off the interest. Bhavita and Mati owe nothing and own their house outright. They believe the short-term struggle was well worth it.

Negotiate with your creditors

If you've got priority debt that you can't afford to pay, not only must you look your debt in the face, you also have to look your lenders in the face. Creditors look far more kindly upon those who take the trouble to explain their situation and seek a solution, rather than just ignoring it. Write to your priority creditors explaining that you are having difficulty with repayments and making it clear that you want to seek a means of settling the debt that's acceptable to both of you. There are sample letters to help you do this on the Citizens Advice Bureau website (http://www.adviceguide.org.uk). You should be able to negotiate an affordable payment plan. If you can only afford £100, not £180, a month, tell them; most would rather have small, regular payments than nothing at all.

Don't delay contacting priority creditors. They have the right to cut off essential services such as your gas and electricity, repossess your belongings or your home and, in the very worst case scenario, take legal action to put you in prison. With this in mind, make sure that you don't agree to pay your other creditors (credit or store card companies, unsecured loans, overdrafts etc.) more than the minimum they require until after you've negotiated an agreement with your priority creditors first.

Negotiate, too, with non-priority creditors if you're struggling to pay their minimum payments. Again, propose a repayment you can afford to stick to and ask each of them to freeze the interest. Any of the free debt advice agencies listed below can help you with all of this.

Debt advice agencies

Always approach one of the free debt advice agencies for help first – rather than a private debt consolidation company. Many of these free agencies will negotiate with lenders on your behalf and can also arrange a debt management plan so that you make a series of single payments which then get divided up and paid on your behalf to each creditor.

Never pay an organisation to work out a debt management plan for you – always use one of the free agencies rather than a private debt consolidation company.

Free debt advice agency contacts

Citizens Advice Bureau

Offers free, independent and confidential advice on a wide range of issues. Your local Citizens Advice Bureau is listed in the phone book or visit their website at www.adviceguide.org.uk

Consumer Credit Counselling Service

Provides free, confidential counselling and money management assistance. Phone 0800 138 1111 or visit their website at www.cccs.co.uk

The National Debtline

Provides free, confidential and independent advice about how to deal with debt problems. Phone 0808 808 4000 or visit their website at www.nationaldebtline.co.uk

Payplan

Debt management and free confidential advice on resolving debt problems. Phone 0800 917 7823 or visit their website at www.payplan.com

Alison's story

It wasn't that Alison didn't earn good money. She just always seemed to end up spending more than she had. If she ran out of money halfway through the month she simply lived on credit. She had no savings and by the time she came to see me her debts had reached a level that was starting to bother her.

Alison was £1,000 overdrawn. She had an £8,000 loan for her car and owed over £5,000 on her credit cards. She seemed shocked that it had got so bad: 'It's not as if I've bought really expensive stuff,' she said. 'Most of it's gone on living: you know, taxis, meals out, makeup and fripperies.'

A close look at Alison's bank statements revealed that her bank charged a £30 fee every time she went past her £500 overdraft limit. This had happened with worrying frequency and her bank charges alone averaged £42 a month. We added this to the interest on her cards and loan and found she was paying £175 each month on the cost of debt. That worked out at £2,000 a year in interest and charges, before she'd even paid back a penny of what she'd borrowed.

When we met next time, Alison amazed me with the economy drive she had already undertaken. 'Superdrug do a skin-care range formulated by Estée Lauder and it's dead cheap,' she announced. 'And I've cancelled my gym membership – I've only been once in three months, so that one aerobics class cost me a hundred and five pounds.'

Alison was serious about keeping to her strict budget for food and entertainment. And she'd cut back significantly on luxuries such as manicures. She had even frozen her credit card. Literally. It was in a block of ice in the back of her freezer. 'So I can only get it in a real emergency,' she laughed.

Alison had negotiated a temporary increase in her overdraft limit to avoid the huge bank charges and switched her credit card debt to a 0 per cent balance transfer deal so it wasn't racking up more interest. She was incredibly buoyed up by her new sense of control. And the cutbacks didn't seem to have dampened her spirit at all. In fact she seemed to get the same kick out of saving money as she'd once got from spending it.

Alison amazed us both by reducing her outgoings by a total of £700 a month – by sticking to this plan she'd be free of her credit card debt and overdraft in just twelve months.

One year on, Alison is completely disciplined about her spending. 'What's weird,' she says, 'is that I don't actually miss any of the things I used to spend my money on – I can't really understand why I did it. I'm so much happier now. I'm far less stressed than I used to be and I love the feeling of being organized and in control.'

As lots of women will testify, getting out of debt leads to feelings of euphoria. Catherine Hardy of the *Telegraph* described her own Sheconomic epiphany after working with Simonne: 'I owed almost twenty-five thousand pounds on credit cards and my financial advisor warned me that I could lose my home if I did not stop spending.' Simonne persuaded Catherine to do the unthinkable: buy toiletries and cleaning products from the Pound Shop, ditch unnecessary insurance policies, cut her food bill from £500 to £350 a month, replace expensive debt with a bank loan and become a compulsive bargain hunter.

Catherine subsequently described herself as a fully paid-up frugalette which, she claims, is now the trendy thing to be.

DO SOMETHING DIFFERENT: MAKE EXTRA MONEY

Try one these ideas and bring in some extra cash:

Use your skills to earn money working from home. If you've got experience in areas such as internet, bookkeeping, administration, marketing, design or writing you can freelance in your free time. Check out the online marketplace for different services: at www.peopleperhour.com you can bid for specific jobs or projects

Work as a TV or film extra Get paid for standing around looking interested. Look into agencies listed on UK Screen's website www.ukscreen.com/agent

Check whether you're entitled to or are claiming the correct amount of tax credit by visiting the Inland Revenue website at www.inlandrevenue.gov.uk/taxcredits or by phoning the tax credit helpline on 0845 300 3900

Reunited with money you may have lost Visit www.mylostaccount.org.uk which will guide you through the process of tracing savings accounts you've lost track of. Or www.thepensionservice.gov.uk/atoz/atozdetailed/pensiontracing.asp for lost pensions. Or pay £18 to search out any lost life policies, pensions, savings or investments for you by visiting www.uar.co.uk

Earn interest on your current account If your current account doesn't pay interest, consider switching to one that does. Use a comparison site like Money Supermarket at www.moneysupermarket.com/currentaccounts to compare the terms. Some will even pay you to come to them.

Visit charity shops in affluent localities Snap up anything with a designer label and then sell it for a super profit on eBay

Take part in market research and get paid for being opinionated in discussion groups, interviews, online surveys etc. Try www.sarosresearch.com

Get paid to shop by using a cash back site before clicking on any online retailers. Try: www.greasypalm.co.uk or www.quidco.com

Host a product party Anything from books to Tupperware or Anne Summers can earn you commission and/or free gifts.

Recover unfair charges deducted by your bank (when you go into unauthorized overdraft), credit card company (when you miss a payment) or your mortgage lender (for extortionate mortgage exit fees).

Or claim compensation if you feel you've been
mis-sold a policy like payment protection insurance.
For ideas how to do this see
www.moneysavingexpert.com

Your debt is unmanageable, what should you do?

Your debt is ugly. The point has come where there's no
hope of paying back what you owe – even if your creditors
agree to cut your monthly payments to the size of a gnat's
asset and freeze the interest. You've explored every
avenue, raided every piggy bank and called in a team of
negotiators to bargain on your behalf. But there's still no
way of paying your debts.

You now have the following options:

The Individual Voluntary Arrangement (IVA)

Option one is to apply for an Individual Voluntary
Arrangement (IVA). This makes your desperate financial
situation official and sets out a formal proposal for paying
back the money you owe in the future. Sometimes,
presented with an IVA, creditors realize they haven't
backed a winner here and may even agree to wipe out
part of your debt.

You have to use an insolvency practitioner to draft the
proposal. He or she then sends it to each of your
creditors. At least 75 per cent of your creditors have to
agree to the proposal for it to be accepted. Once it's

agreed, that's it. They can't ask you to pay back more of your debt, or clear it more quickly. Your insolvency practitioner then oversees the payments.

Going down the IVA route is a less dramatic alternative to bankruptcy – the second of your options – and there are fewer, but still some, stigmas attached. It will leave a nasty stain on your credit file for six years, which won't help your credit rating. Once the IVA has expired, if you need credit again some lenders won't want to know you. And, because you're a bit of a financial pariah, you could be charged a higher rate of interest than someone with a good credit rating. IVAs can also be very expensive – running into thousands of pounds – and getting agreement from your creditors can be time-consuming.

Bankruptcy

There are few nice things to say about bankruptcy. It's even a horrible word – all hard with sharp edges, whereas solvency sounds kind of fluid and silky. More importantly, being declared bankrupt affects all areas of your life. You could be barred from some jobs, need court permission for others, or you could lose your possessions and face complications with credit for six years.

But bankruptcy is also a right you have in law. If you're being relentlessly pursued for money you haven't got, and there's no other option, you can declare yourself bankrupt.

Otherwise, a creditor can apply for your bankruptcy. Being bankrupt means you stand to lose any assets owned or part owned by you although, nowadays, you're unlikely to lose the roof over your head. Also, it kind of goes without saying that bankruptcy doesn't do much for your credit rating either.

Always consider IVAs and bankruptcy only as a last resort. Find out about the full implications of these processes by talking to one of the free debt advice agencies listed on page 204 or to the Insolvency Service www.insolvency.gov.uk

Bankruptcy might be the only means left to you to face your debts. If it happens, though, it's not the end of the world and you can move on from it. We know a wealthy businessman who has four bankruptcy orders, all acquired when he was trying to 'make it' in his early years, framed on his office wall. He has them there to remind himself, and his staff, never to fear failure but to see it as an opportunity to learn.

So let's not leave on a bad note. Remember, if you have debt look it in the face and deal with it. Follow the advice in this chapter, take responsibility and enlist the free help of some of the agencies. And don't forget that, used wisely, debt can turn you into a top-notch Sheconomist!

My Sheconomics Checklist
Law 5

How are you doing on looking debt in the face?   ✓

I know how much I owe and have a plan to repay it	
I understand the difference between good debt and bad debt	
I'm not afraid to take on good debt but avoid bad debt	
I pay off my credit card in full every month	
I'm happy to negotiate with creditors to reduce the interest they charge	
I'm willing to Do Something Different to be debt-free	

Your Sheconomics debt-payment plan table

List of people you owe money to	Balance due	Minimum payment each month	APR	Priority debt	What you plan to pay each month
	£	£	%	Y or N	£
	£	£	%	Y or N	£
	£	£	%	Y or N	£
	£	£	%	Y or N	£
	£	£	%	Y or N	£
	£	£	%	Y or N	£
	£	£	%	Y or N	£
	£	£	%	Y or N	£
	£	£	%	Y or N	£
	£	£	%	Y or N	£
	£	£	%	Y or N	£
	£	£	%	Y or N	£
Total	£	£			£

Chapter 7
Law 6: Share Financial Intimacies

'I am always amazed by the way that
couples are happy to mingle their body fluids
but are cautious about mingling their money.'

Andrew Marshall (marital therapist and author of
I Love You But I'm Not In Love With You).

When it comes to intimacy no one can touch my friend
Louise. She hasn't found The One yet, but at the age of
thirty-six she's really giving her all when it comes to pinning
down Mr Right. When she has a date her evenings are
planned to perfection: the wine's chilled, the candles are
flickering, the lamb noisettes would make Nigella proud,
Lionel Richie croons from the stereo and scattered on the
dining table are . . . all her cheque stubs, receipts and
bank statements.

There's no getting away from it, money's just not romantic.
When it comes to passion killers it's probably on a par with
big pants. But let's face it, if your relationship has reached
a point where your toothbrushes are cohabiting and your
plans extend beyond next weekend, you just can't ignore
finance.

So many of us are scared to bare all when it comes to money. But financial intimacy does mean exposing all your money secrets to another person. So you might be feeling you'd rather turn the light off and not mention it.

But does it make sense to be secretive about what we earn or what we owe? Why are we cagey about what we can and can't afford? Money secrets are the kiss of death to any close relationship – whether it's with a partner, spouse, business partner, close friend or even yourself. Yes, you have to be open and honest with yourself too. That means denial has to go out the window.

In this chapter we'll show you how to get up close and financially personal with yourself and your loved ones. We'll talk through how you can explore your money mindset, and that of your loved ones. We'll help you ensure that money doesn't pop up and sabotage your life at any stage – that's whether you're on a first date or coping with the arrival of a new generation of big spenders: your children.

By sharing financial intimacies you'll be:

- Comfortable talking to others about money
- Able to plan towards future goals with a partner
- Confident enough to raise any money issues with your friends or partner without getting emotionally charged

- Intimate with your money mindset
- Respectful of your own needs and financial limitations and not led by others
- Fully informed about financial matters that relate to both you and, where appropriate, your partner

First date: when do you pop the M word?
When you're still enjoying the magical early days of a relationship, the subject of money is probably the last thing you want to bring up. Jonathan Self, author of *Teaching Teenagers about Money* thinks it's never too early to mention the M word. Even on a first date! But surely checking out his financial credentials when you've just met is as tactless as turning up in a wedding dress with three bridesmaids in tow. And just as likely to send him running.

However, that doesn't mean the M word is off your agenda altogether. Some money moments on the first date have to be faced – like who's going to pay, for example. According to a National Savings 2008 survey 40 per cent of men expect to pick up the bill on a date. Yet, bless 'em, the guys are reaching for their wallets from chivalry rather than women's expectations. Because, in fact, only 17 per cent of women expect the man to pay. On the other hand, that doesn't mean men aren't looking for a return on their investment. Nearly a fifth of men in the survey said they'd end a relationship if they didn't think it was worth the expense.

For all our supposed equality, when we eat out today the bill still usually lands on the guy's side of the table. Don't pretend it's not there. At that early stage, mention the unmentionable; then a number of scenarios could follow:

a) He confesses to having come out without any money/being broke/assuming you would pay . . . You won't hear the rest because you'll be getting your coat.

b) He insists on paying in return for your divine company. One of the fab 40 per cent!

c) He agrees to split the bill. He's either a bit frugal or doesn't want to appear chauvinistic. He's definitely in with a chance.

Believe us, further down the line, if you've made a commitment to a future together, you're going to be popping the M word on a regular basis.

Presents
Another money moment that's likely to pop up early concerns presents. What happens when you've only been going out for weeks or months and a birthday – or Christmas – comes along?

That 'Do I get him a present' dilemma is a tricky one. If you do proffer a pressie and he doesn't give you one back, the embarrassment stakes are high. On the other hand, let's say you've assumed the two of you aren't on gift-giving terms yet. Then, out of the blue, your empty-handedness is met by a lavish offering from him. Eek! That can be just as mortifying. The price of getting it wrong feels huge in emotional terms. But it doesn't have to be.

If a gifting gaffe leaves you red-faced you'll need a good sense of humour to rescue you. Or you could turn your lapse into a way of complimenting him – 'The last time I bought a guy a present he dumped me, so I thought it might be safer not to.' Even better if you can laugh together about the daftness of it all. Just don't fall into the trap of judging the relationship by what he buys you. Or by how much he spends on you.

When it comes to presents for friends, be careful not to start something you'd rather you hadn't. When my friend Dawn and I (Karen) were both first-time mums, she appeared at Christmas time with a small present for my son. To assuage my guilt, I nipped out later that day and bought a slightly more expensive gift for her daughter. Before I knew it we were into that whole buying-for-the-children thing, every Christmas and every birthday. Trouble is, she went on to have five more children (cue christening presents) whereas I only had one more (and no christenings). Before you could say Toys R Us I was buying twelve kiddie gifts a year just for her lot.

Finally, Dawn had the common sense to put a stop to it, something I should have done years before but I was too scared of appearing mean. If you're sucked into reciprocal buying for the sake of it then, whatever you do, pluck up the nerve to knock it on the head. The other person will probably be hugely relieved that you did.

Sun, sea and saving

As you trip off down the tunnel of love together the financial stuff is ever-present. Who pays for the holiday, for example? Maybe one of you will take the 'What the hell' approach and shove the cost on yet another credit card. That's deeply worrying because it could spell trouble that lasts much longer than your tan.

Planning a holiday together is the perfect opportunity to chat about your spending and savings priorities. Far better to know up-front whether his idea of luxury is your idea of no-frills. The more you can talk about things and plan together as a couple, the better. If you just leave things to chance then you can't really complain that you'd rather have had two weeks herding yaks in Patagonia when he's booked a fortnight at his mum and dad's caravan in Norfolk.

The same goes for weekends away or holidays with friends. Say in a weak moment you agree to join your best mate on a week's holiday boozing and clubbing in Ibiza but you're still trying to pay for last year's holiday with your already over-stretched credit card. Be openly honest about what is and what isn't realistically possible for you and find cheaper ways of spending time together.

Five Top Tips For Affordable Holidays

1. **You can holiday on the cheap** if you're prepared to forego a few five-star treats. More people are trying flashpacking (affluent backpacking) or hostelling (www.hostelworld.com), cultural exchanges where you do farm work in exchange for accommodation (www.helpx.net), staying with hosts abroad (www.couchsurfing.com) or swapping homes with people who'd like to holiday in your home while you holiday in theirs (www.guardianhomeexchange.co.uk).

2. **Get free flights** by collecting air miles. Some credit cards give you air miles when you take out the card and whenever you spend. Look into whether you can earn a holiday from your spending.

3. **Travel insurance may be an optional extra** You can cover medical costs in the EU member countries with a European Health Insurance Card (free from

ehic.org.uk or your post office). Your home contents
and private health policies may also cover you when
travelling abroad. Check your policy before buying
more insurance.

4. **Budget for your holiday** Decide in advance how
   much you can afford to spend while you're away.
   Break the budget down into a spend-per-day amount
   and stick to it. Take travellers cheques rather than
   your credit card – some make hefty charges when
   you use them abroad.

5. **If you take your mobile abroad, don't text**
   Although legislation has made the cost of EU mobile
   calls cheaper, the rules don't cover texts. And turn off
   your voicemail service or you'll get charged as much
   as if you'd made a call. And if the caller called you,
   remember if you're abroad you are the one who pays
   for the call.

Friends – and money envy

An earnings gap can put even the very best friendships
under strain and produce huge doses of envy – like where
one of you has more spare change rattling around in the
bottom of her Prada handbag than the other earns in a
week, or where the minted one is moaning about rising
school fees while the skinted one is applying for free
school meals. Even the closest of chums will feel a spot of

'frienvy' when there's a magnum-sized gulf between each other's spending power.

It needn't be a big deal-breaker if your friends have more money than you. Just don't even try to keep up with them, that's all. Come clean about the meagreness of your income.

Try and be sensitive to your friends' financial status, too, and never, ever make assumptions about what they can afford. There's nothing worse than the 'kind' friend who tells you she's moved hell and high water to get you a ticket to a charity bash and casually lets slip that you owe her £200 for it. Check what your friends are prepared to spend on a meal out before booking the priciest restaurant in town. And, whatever you do, never go into debt for the sake of keeping up with high-earning friends.

Money envy isn't only the domain of the financially challenged. Apparently even those with a few million secured under their diamond-studded belts still turn the bright green eye of envy towards David Beckham or Roman Abramovich for their even wealthier lifestyles. It seems that whatever the size of their personal fortune, the competitive coveter will always want more. Just goes to show that how rich you feel has relatively little to do with how much money you've got.

Monica's story

For Monica, a thirty-two year-old freelance journalist, money has always meant she can treat her friends and express her feelings for other people. Monica's the kind of girl who gives you an embarrassingly expensive handbag for your birthday, when all you gave her was a scented candle. She's also unbelievably generous on a night out with the girls. Before you turn up at the bar she's ordered champagne and paid for it. At the end of a meal she's likely to sneak off as if she's going to the loo, then you find the bill's been settled.

Not surprisingly, Monica is very popular. But, the fact is, her friends would like her even if she wasn't so generous. So they were shocked to discover recently that Monica has huge debts and has been spending way beyond her means for ages.

All her life, her friends' perception of her had driven Monica's behaviour. Her mother had made 'keeping up appearances' a personal crusade and impressed on Monica that you should always make other people think you were doing well. But when the debts got too much Monica had to brace herself and reveal the grim reality of her financial situation to her friends. A tough call.

But her friends didn't drop her, as she'd dreaded. Instead, they rallied round with sympathy and understanding. In fact, they'd never before felt closer to Monica. She had become a real person, with real money issues – just like them.

Monica faced up to the fact that she'd been using money as a route to friendship. She was able to talk about it and now, as a fully-fledged Sheconomist, she's stripped money of the old significance it had for her and has begun to enjoy a healthy money-relationship and a more secure future. And she likes nothing more than a good night out with her friends – so long as it's on the cheap.

Settling down together: whose money is it anyway?

Three quarters of couples in Britain find money the hardest subject to talk about with their partners according to a recent survey by the Financial Services Authority (FSA). More than a quarter of couples regularly argue when they try to discuss their finances; about a third lie to their partners about how much they spend on their credit cards and more than a third are kept awake at night worrying about their money situation. According to Relate, debt and money worries are the prime cause of relationship breakdown in more than 70 per cent of cases.

Money is neither sexy nor romantic, nevertheless the dream partnership has to be one where you can talk together about absolutely anything. If you're in a committed relationship where certain topics are off the agenda then, sorry to have to tell you this, but you're probably with the wrong person.

Even in the most communicative of relationships, let's be honest, raising a taboo subject can be a bit tricky. Money differences can wreak havoc in any relationship and they are the number one reason for divorce. So, if you're planning to live together happily, financial compatibility is as vital as sexual compatibility and you need to be able to discuss both. Later in this chapter we'll show you how to have those money conversations without all hell breaking loose. See page 238 **Having an argument-free money conversation**.

Joint accounts

If you'll be running up bills together you have to sort out from the start how you are going to pay for them. The time has come to talk about joint accounts. In fact, joint accounts are on the decrease and for a number of reasons including more second marriages and more transitory relationships.

Then there's trust, or lack of it. It's a human trait to underestimate our own spending and to keep a much keener eye on what the other person spends. If either of you is prone to this bias you could be heading for joint account friction. Equally, if the idea of merging your finances with your life partner horrifies you because you don't really trust them, then why are you committing your life to an untrustworthy individual? It could be time to move on. The money mindset exercise on page 232 will help you identify such feelings.

Joint earners have to sort out whether everything will go into one account, or whether to keep some healthy distance. Some couples set up a joint account to cover shared expenses – mortgage, household bills and the like – plus each has a separate account for personal spending: a three-pot system – yours, mine, ours. You could have another 'ours' pot (account) to cover things like holidays, saving for the wedding or the deposit on a property, or multiple pots, whatever suits. Salaries go into the personal accounts with a set amount transferred into the joint account(s) each month.

If you opt for this approach, decide exactly what are joint expenses and how much you need to cover them. Either work on a 50:50 basis, or in proportion to each other's net pay. So if one brings home £1,500 a month and the other £2,000, a 40:60 split would be fair.

We can't be prescriptive about this. If you and your partner have a friction-free system that you're both perfectly happy with – one that's based on trust and generosity, then you're already doing the right thing. But if one partner is niggled about the unfairness of your arrangement, some renegotiation would be advisable.

Five Top Tips For Joint Account Harmony

1. Pay in a set, agreed amount every month This should cover the monthly costs on your home, utilities and any other expenses you've agreed to share. You could add on extra to create a financial cushion in case of emergencies (e.g. the central heating breaking down) or to cover the occasional shared treat (e.g. a weekend away).

2. Make the contribution fair If one of you is earning more than the other a 50:50 split might be unfair. The higher earner should consider contributing the greater proportion.

3. Agree what the joint account covers Monthly utility bills will be clear-cut, variable expenditure less so. If you both use the account for food, booze, treats, travel etc., agree what a reasonable monthly spend should be.

4. Review it together regularly Sit down at least once a month and go through the paperwork. Check that what you're paying in is keeping pace with your outgoings. Make sure you're both aware of your expenses and financial commitments.

5. If one partner isn't happy with the arrangement discuss it in a calm and neutral way. Whatever happens, don't get into competitive or revenge spending. Remember you're both liable if the account goes overdrawn.

It's alarming how many women confess to keeping a stash of RAM (Running Away Money) in a secret account. This is probably the epitome of financial adultery. If you have your own RAM hoard, ask yourself what's at the root of it. Is lack of autonomy an issue? Are you protecting yourself in case of a break-up? Do you resent the fact that your partner controls your spending? Squirrelling money away isn't always the answer. Try addressing the imbalance by starting a money conversation in one of the ways suggested on page 238. Or perhaps consider getting some relationship counselling.

The spends that 'don't really count'
One trainee Sheconomist found that having a joint account made her feel she had unlimited funds. Her

spending became totally reckless and out of control. After finding themselves overdrawn every month, she and her partner agreed she should have a separate account for her 'spending' money. That way she'd have a set budget and would keep her hands off the main account.

But it didn't work, and she continued to spend on herself from the couple's main account: she found herself playing games with what really counted as hers and what she could justify as household spending. She fell into the trap of thinking certain spends 'didn't really count' and developed quite a talent for deluding herself. Resentment towards her husband built up too because, she complained, 'He doesn't seem to count his outgoings in the same way as he counts my shoes.'

Our trainee Sheconomist is far from unusual. Lots of us delude ourselves, to a greater or lesser extent, when it comes to what does and doesn't 'count'. Here are a few to set you thinking next time you're shopping:

- Supermarket shopping: Those few CDs and cosmetics that you pop into the trolley. Do they ever become disguised as part of the weekly shop?

- Airport shopping: A purse plumped up with euros, dollars, whatever, fools you into thinking that expensive perfume, the new watch and those four pairs of flip-flops are part of the holiday. And foreign currency feeds our play-money delusions and beliefs such as, 'Only 50 dinadoodas, that's cheap!!!'.

• Internet shopping: You're ordering a book online for your child's homework project and before you can say 'click here to buy' you've ordered yourself a new iPod.

DO SOMETHING DIFFERENT: TAKE A MONEY REALITY CHECK

Are you and your partner both equally savvy about how much money comes in and goes out of your accounts?

Try, each of you separately, writing down the amounts for general income and expenses from the list below – then compare figures and see who's closest to reality.

HOW MUCH IS?
• The total amount paid INTO your joint account each month
• The amount paid out on your mortgage
• The total amount (excluding the mortgage) of joint debt you have
• The cost of one month's food
• The amount spent each month on eating out
• The total monthly cost of the household utility bills

If you're more than a few pounds out, or if only one of you knows the answers to these questions, it's time to take a closer look at what's going on between you financially.

Getting to know you – and getting to know your money mindset

Early on in your relationship you should explore each other's money mindsets and find out if you're both singing from the same balance sheet. A cash-confessional is good for the soul and a must for wiping away those feelings of worry that money induces. Unearth the role money plays in each other's life and chip away at the meaning each of you attaches to money.

Hang on, you might be thinking, do we *really* want to go there? While it's human nature to follow the path of least resistance, try and see this as a chance to deepen your relationship and to make sure neither of you is harbouring any illusions. To find out sooner rather than later if, when he said he'd share everything with you, he meant his humungous debts and abysmal credit rating!

Here, we've come up with some money mindset questions for you and your partner to discuss together. This exercise throws up the variety of meanings that money has for different people. It also demands unflinching honesty. Money mindsets are as individual as our fingerprints. We all come with different genes, histories, personalities and experiences. Accept this. Listen to your partner's stories and views. Then see if you can make any connections between your money mindsets and any current relationship issues.

Most importantly, when you chat over your answers together, suppress any desire to judge each other. Just congratulate yourselves on being able to own up to who you are financially.

This exercise is also worthwhile even if you're not in an intimate relationship – talk through the questions together with a friend, or share your money mindset feelings in company on a girls' night in.

Think about the questions below then chat over your answers and what you think they reveal.

Uncover your money mindset

- What are your money memories as a child? Try to share one story each about your childhood money memories.
- What money messages did you learn from your parents or guardians? Does a particular 'saying' come to mind?
- What does money mean to you now?
- How do you feel about debt?
- What's your definition of being wealthy?
- What would you do with a big windfall?
- What do you think of people who make a lot of money?
- What would it take for you to feel financially secure?

Come to terms with your money history

One trainee Sheconomist puts her money difficulties down to growing up in a very low-income household. Throughout her childhood money was scarce and food was always in short supply. Now she is absolutely obsessed with keeping her cupboards stocked to the brim. Running out of anything throws her into a panic.

Another girl has the opposite history. She grew up in a home where money was plentiful and everyone spent with wanton abandon. Now she feels she has no grasp on the value of money, or the consequences of spending, and fears losing control completely.

How much of your present limiting money behaviour is a hangover from your past? As we discussed in chapter two, a hoarding tendency may be the result of a scarcity mindset rooted in childhood experience, or money talk may cause anxiety because your parents always acted as if financial meltdown was imminent. You or your partner may have grown up in a family where money was never talked about. Or with parents who only expressed love through money and material gifts. Maybe one parent worried incessantly and this made the other more secretive. Thus, exhuming family skeletons from the cupboard may well help uncover why you each have different habits and beliefs about money.

Accept this. Recognize that childhood money memories may spill over into current money mindsets and that understanding and coming to terms with these memories is the first step towards liberating yourself and your partner from the grip of infantile attitudes to money.

One trainee Sheconomist confesses to having a dismally immature relationship with money: she simply lands all her worrying about money at her husband's door. Another feels she always has to compensate for her husband's overspending: she is constantly infuriated by his 'child-like' behaviour with money.

Accept the past and be prepared to shed it and move on. When you and your partner understand each other's different money histories you can work with it and not let it put a strain on your relationship. Having a shared understanding means you're more likely to tolerate each other's differences and to be prepared to compromise where necessary.

Don't forget that different personality traits play a role, too: extroverts are more comfortable with borrowing; introverts would rather save for something than go into debt; emotionally stable individuals find it easier to follow plans and budgets than do the emotionally fragile. One partner might have stronger self-control than the other and, therefore, be better at delaying gratification. Help each other by being understanding. Some personality traits are probably pretty much set in stone, others may temper, but by talking openly about money you'll understand each other's spending and saving priorities and styles.

Gender can have a bearing, too: men and women often vary in the level of risk they'll accept – in general, men are more comfortable with higher levels of risk when making investment decisions, for example, or the size of mortgage they'll take on. And women tend to like their money to be visible, so may prefer to invest in property rather than shares. Compromises can be reached, but only if you each know where the other's coming from.

How well do you and your partner communicate about money matters?

Opposites, they say, attract but they can also clash in pretty uncomfortable ways. One trainee Sheconomist has been married for twenty years to a man who's as conservative as she is extravagant and they still can't agree about spending and saving. She racks up more and more credit card bills, which launches him into a state of high anxiety, causing her to feel guilt and shame. Then she justifies it to herself by saying that they earn enough and that he doesn't show her enough attention, anyhow. The real issue here is her need for his affection and his inability to give it, but this is something they have never discussed.

Conversely, one of our top Sheconomists described how she was and always had been a real money worrier when she went into her relationship, but talking and getting her feelings out in the open to a supportive partner really helped her. Feeling loved gave her a sense of worthiness for the things she wanted. Her lover showed her that the really special things in life weren't sitting on a shop shelf or hanging on the rails.

Do you have a communication problem?

Answer yes or no to the following statements:

1. We regularly sit down and assess our financial situation
2. We each know what the other earns and spends
3. Neither of us tries to control the spending of the other
4. We know what each other's financial dreams and goals for the future are
5. We're quite happy and relaxed discussing money
6. We never argue about money
7. I know the role that money played in my partner's life as he/she was growing up
8. We both know what savings, investments and pensions we have
9. We are both equally aware of our household running costs and expenses
10. We take equal responsibility for financial management and decision-making

How did you do? If you answered yes to all ten, or nine, sounds like you've got a healthy and honest money relationship. Yes to between five and eight and you're doing OK but you need to communicate more and improve that score. If you answered yes to fewer than five statements, you could be heading for trouble. You may, for example, need to increase the degree of shared involvement in money matters, or you may be hiding things from each other – a recipe for relationship and/or financial disaster. You need to head off future problems by talking more openly, working out a joint strategy and doing the Having an argument-free money conversation exercise below.

How to have an argument-free money conversation

'Of all the icy blasts that blow on love, a request for money is the most chilling and havoc-wreaking.' So says Gustave Flaubert's heroine in his novel *Madame Bovary*. Emma Bovary clearly needed our advice on how to talk about money.

That 'chilling' conversation needn't be as difficult as you think. But you do need to pick the right time, catch someone unawares and they're likely to respond defensively; and select your words carefully, ill-expressed, anything you might say has the potential to trigger an explosive conversation.

Five Top Tips for Constructive Conversation

1. Choose the right time and place

Set a mutually covenient time and place to talk about money. Try and avoid holding it late at night when you're likely to be tired. Do your best to minimize the chances of being disturbed – perhaps wait until the children are in bed? Make it regular, but be flexible, if one of you is in a bad mood it's unlikely you'll have a constructive conversation.

2. Agree the ground rules

Agree the ground rules you need to suit your situation, but good rules which apply to everyone are:

- No interruptions while the other person is talking
- Definitely no blaming the other person
- Explain your position in a calm manner, leaving emotions aside
- Start and finish by saying at least one positive thing about the way your partner handles money, especially if you know there are sensitivities

3. Work as a team

Make a pact that you'll work together to sort out any financial problems you have. This means ensuring each of you has equal information about the financial situation and is equally committed.

4. Get organized

Have a system for storing your paperwork and both use it. Keep some kind of household budget (or spending plan) and review it together regularly.

5. Stick to the subject

If you're discussing a money issue, keep the conversation strictly to that. Don't get sidetracked into bringing up other grievances. Money is a barometer of the health of your relationship. And money arguments can be a symptom of some deeper relationship issues that you need to address separately.

Financing the family

There's no denying that having children changes everything. Relate tell us that couples with children are four times more likely to fight about money than those without. Children have a tsunami-like capability to devastate a financial relationship. So planning a baby means planning how you're going to manage financially too.

The arrival of a baby often means the loss of one salary. Adopt the right attitude to this. In one sense you are still both working full time, the only difference is that now one of you gets the income. It needn't necessarily be the wage-earner who controls the money or keeps the lion's share of it. Talk all this over as soon as your pregnancy test is positive.

You'll need to sort out whether the one who stays at home will get an 'income' from the other or whether one joint account will serve you both. And if you are taking a career break, consider asking your partner to continue to pay into a pension for you (at the time of writing, an earning spouse in the UK can pay up to £3,600 a year into a partner's pension). That way you won't lose a key part of your financial independence while you're spending time in Nappy Valley.

Putting our children first

Think carefully about the role children will have in your financial life in the future. Through the ages women have been the ones who made the sacrifices. We're often brought up to put others before ourselves, sometimes to our own detriment. Lots of us are skilled in the art of lavishing money on others yet feel guilty spending on ourselves. This is especially true when it comes to children. Being a mother doesn't have to mean being a money martyr.

Of course, every mum wants her children to have more opportunities than she had herself. It's also natural to want to protect them from misery, disaster and disappointment. But this is crippling many families financially.

There's one financial favour you can do your children as they grow up. Set a good example: show them some real sound money sense. For example, don't let them see you being wantonly wasteful. ('Mummy ate all the leftover chocolate because it was near its sell-by date' is worth a try.) Also make sure you're not conveying the wrong messages. ('Mummy loves Daddy for his bonus.') If children see their parents constantly drooling over and amassing consumer goods, they'll assume that the secret to eternal bliss lies within the pages of the *Argos* catalogue, or that a new kitchen and garden makeover is some kind of marriage therapy.

How you talk about money will send signals to children, too. The more neutral you can be when you and your other half discuss money, the less chance that your children will have a dysfunctional relationship with it later on in their lives. Extreme anxiety, recklessness, fear or secrecy about money all get drip-fed down to children and any of these can set them up for a tough time as adults.

Relentlessly teach your children about the seductive and pernicious power of advertising; explain that marketers are out to get their money. Believe it or not, children under the age of about ten don't always realize this. In their innocent worlds adults don't lie so they believe every word the advertisers tell them. Help them to spot all the sneaky ways advertisers try to create desire or sell us a dream.

Aside from advertisers trying to part them from their money (and yours), as they grow older your children will come up against peer pressure, too. This will result in them persistently trying to bamboozle you into buying the latest phone, computer game or trainers. The best weapon to help them resist peer pressure is to build their self-esteem. The higher they rate their self-worth, the less vulnerable they are to manipulation by others. Tell them how wonderful they are on the *in*side and point out to them the good personal qualities you see in others, rather than what they wear or own.

You'll also have to practise saying the N (for NO) word quite a bit. But also, instead of batting them off with 'We can't afford that', challenge them to think of ways to afford things by shopping around, searching for good deals or swapping or selling unwanted stuff.

Here are our other top tips for managing these mini-muggers:

- Don't lavish money on babies. In the first few months they have trouble picking out their mum from other humans. There's no way they can tell if they're wearing

Osh Kosh or Oxfam. Your buggy doesn't need to attract more admiring glances than your baby.

- Give pocket money from around the age of five or six. Make it a fixed amount given on a set day, with no strings attached but also no hand-outs in between. It's an early way for children to learn about the finite nature of money and that it has to last until next pay day.

- Encourage children to save, too, even if it's just putting 20ps in a jar. And to wait until birthdays or Christmas for extra treats. The better they are at delaying gratification, the more adept they'll be at handling money as adults.

- Be careful about paying (or bribing) children to do chores. They should help with washing up, keep their rooms tidy, clean their shoes etc. as their contribution to the household. If you give them money for doing things they should do anyway, you'll end up even paying them to get out of bed.

- Make them aware that the household has to run on a budget. And that you all have to stick to it and prune it when necessary. Let them help you choose the best-value buys in the supermarket. Tell older children the limit you'll pay for a holiday, give them a list of everyone's requirements and let them shop around to find the best deal.

- Don't inflict your money worries on the children. Making them aware does not mean waving the water rates bill under the nose of your six year old. There's nothing they can do about it.

- Give older children (twelve and over) an allowance. I (Karen) found giving them the family allowance worked well. They had to buy everything they needed from this, apart from school uniform, shoes and a good winter coat, which I'd buy. It's amazing how those expensive trainers (that *everyone* else had and without which they could *never show their face* to their mates again) suddenly become less of a priority when they're buying.

- Teach your children about the value of money from an early age and the ride through the teenage years won't be too bumpy. Accept that their attitude will challenge you at times and leave you downright speechless at others. The book *Get Out of My Life: But First take me and Alex Into Town* by Anthony Wolf and Suzanne Franks sums it up beautifully – although the words '*and give me a tenner*' would make the perfect subtitle.

- Work. OK, we don't send children up chimneys any more but from the age of fourteen they can work part-time and should be encouraged to do so.

Expensive nest syndrome

In coaching I (Simonne) have encountered women coming up to retirement who are still bailing out their adult children. Their immature offspring have got so used to being taken care of they're like toddlers, struggling to stand on their own two feet. These huge cuckoos that won't leave the nest, or keep popping back for more, put women (and men, too) at financial risk.

Lots of women have woefully inadequate provision for the future anyway, without also bolstering up their children's finances. Or, even worse, they're amassing debts that will take years to shed, long after the time when the children should be taking care of themselves. Know when to cut the umbilical cash-cord and set them free.

Planning your future together

Whatever your financial situation, if you're planning to make a life together it's worth checking out what financial security means to each of you. For example, one trainee Sheconomist told us how she feels completely secure and content with her and her partner's savings, but knows that her partner always feels they're one step away from poverty.

Another couple, Mike and Laura, had built up sizeable joint savings. But it was only when they'd had a proper discussion about their finances that it transpired that each had different plans for them. Laura thought she was putting money into their nest egg so she could stop work and start having children, Mike thought they were saving for a new Aston Martin. That's why it's so important to break the great taboo and get your money beliefs out in the open before crunch-times come and the truth (or something in the garage) catches you by surprise.

Whether you're planning to get married, buy a semi or ditch life in Dulwich to discover Delhi, reach agreement about your goals and discuss how you're going to meet them. If one of you is in debt, for example, you'll need to have a serious heart-to-heart about how you're going to work together to pay it off.

We're all for merging as much as possible in a relationship but you wouldn't want to be saddled with your partner's poor credit rating. His unsavoury past might include bad debts or missed mortgage payments and these could come back and haunt your combined finances. A way round this is to keep separate accounts. Did you know that if one of you overspends on the joint account you are both fully liable for the whole balance? Holding up your hands and saying 'It wasn't me, sir' unfortunately won't get you a let-off. So, if you love him but not his undesirable ways with money, keep some or all of your finances separate. It'll also ensure you don't have a problem applying for credit in the future.

Even if you choose to pool your finances, there are some financial products that you can't merge. Pensions and ISAs, for example, can be held in only one person's name. You can even save tax if an account is held in one name – that of whoever pays less tax – rather that both, so joint isn't always best.

To reiterate: the important thing is to know what plans each of you has and to link them to your common goals.

If you stop work to have children don't forget to rethink how you own your assets. For example, if you both have investment portfolios it could be worth transferring all of them into the non-earner's name. That way you'll be able to make the most of the tax-free personal allowance (at the time of writing, £6,035 a year for under sixty-five year olds). The transfer won't be liable for capital gains tax either because it will be treated as a 'gift' (there, that's Christmas taken care of, too!).

People are marrying, or choosing to live together, later now, often when they're well into their thirties. That means both partners may already own a property when they get together. If you're in this lucky position and decide to keep both jointly, one to live in and one as an investment, you'll need to nominate one as your primary residence. It's usually best to nominate the property you live in so that you don't have to pay capital gains tax on the increase in value when you come to sell.

Partial exemption from capital gains tax applies to the other property for the period that it was the main residence for one of you plus a further three years. And there's another exemption, called private letting relief, which exempts a further £40,000 of the gain when you sell. All of which means it may make sense to keep the property you let out in the name of the original owner, rather than joint names. You'll need to get advice on this.

Your decision to marry, or register your civil partnership, can be influenced as much by finance as it can by romance. Take inheritance tax, for example. One trainee Sheconomist and her partner found themselves rushing to make an emergency appointment at the registry office because they'd suddenly found out that, if either of them were to die, the survivor would get clobbered with a huge inheritance tax bill. They'd been together for eighteen years and shared a property for fifteen years. All that time they'd lived together, however, counts for nothing when it comes to inheritance tax. Only legally recognized spouses are exempt from the tax. Although they'd always baulked at the idea of marriage, within six weeks this couple had tied the knot.

There may be trouble ahead . . .

We don't want to rain on your romance parade but you never know when you and your partner's financial relationship might take a hit. Job losses, mortgage rate rises and babies are just a few of the bombshells that could deal your bank balance a blow. But the impact of these can be softened by a strong relationship with the channels of communication kept firmly open.

You can't guard against everything but you should be proactive about legalities and property arrangements. If you're getting together with someone later in life, you're likely to be bringing more assets to the relationship. Once you're living together a solicitor can draw up a partnership agreement to protect you legally in case of a break up. If you're sharing a home and contributing towards the mortgage, make sure the property is in joint names. We can't all count on marrying an ex-Beatle without a pre-nup.

You can still hang on to some financial independence, too, by keeping an account in your own name. It's also a good idea to build up a credit rating in your own name.

In a healthy relationship both partners should have equal access to money and to the facts about their financial status. An all-too-common practice is that one partner handles all money issues. But what if the person who shuns all the financial stuff is left alone, through death, divorce or some other unforeseen disaster? What if that person was you?

We've heard of lots of cases of older women who are widowed suddenly and have no idea where the paperwork is kept, or even how to write out a cheque. Make sure that's not you by getting involved now. Time to start swotting up and keeping abreast of where the money's going. Pluck up the courage to look at the bank statements. Try a minor flirtation with the financial news pages now and again. You'll find it's really not as scary as you thought.

Or if you're the one who finds it hard to release your iron grip on the purse strings, try involving your other half in more money decisions. Share out the handling of the finances between you and put aside time to talk about them.

For better or worse – what do you know?

It's never too early to make sure you are fully informed about:

- What you both own and owe. Do you know, for example, which of your assets and liabilities are in joint names?
- The pension arrangement each of you has – employer schemes and any private plans paid into
- What the pensions would pay out in the event of long-term disability or death
- The state pension each of you can expect to get
- If there's a big age difference between you, how you plan to manage your finances once the first one retires
- If only one of you has a pension, what dying after retiring would mean for the surviving partner
- The status of your wills. If you have children under eighteen, who would be their legal guardians in the event of your death
- The cover each of you has through your employers and any private insurances protecting you against long-term illness, disability or death.
- Whether you've nominated each other as beneficiary on any insurance plan, including any endowment policies and employer life cover

Secrets and Lies

You may not be living a lie but who hasn't at some time been economical with the truth about their spending? You know the kind of thing – like saying that the astronomically priced outfits you've just bought for the children were in the sale. Or shoving all the packaging from your new, expensive make-up into the bottom of the bin.

Are they harmless white lies or the rocky road to something more serious? Recent retail research in the US shows that more and more women are paying for expensive designer goods with cash – so they can hide how much they spend. They may think they're harmlessly pulling the wool over their partner's eyes but it's really a kind of financial adultery.

And it's not just spends that we're keeping secret from our partners. Many women keep their savings or investments hush-hush too, often because they don't want their partner getting their hands on them.

DO SOMETHING DIFFERENT: SEE WHAT YOUR BANK STATEMENT SAYS ABOUT YOU

Open your bank statements when they arrive and look at the account summary box (which is usually at the top of the front page). This tells you the balance you started with at the beginning of the month (the opening balance) and the amount at the end (the closing balance). Also look at total payments in and total payments out of your account. Confront whether you're spending more than you have coming in. If you have a partner and share this account, do this exercise together.

Then take a pen and label each expense on the statement as 'necessity', 'emotional purchase', 'sensible' or 'moment of madness'. Add up the totals to show you how much you spend on each category. This will reveal where the majority of your money is going and on what kind of spending. Be open with each other and plan together any changes that are necessary.

It's not uncommon for clients to ask me (Simonne) never to call their home phone, or only to contact them at their place of work so their partner needn't know they're seeking support with their finances. Of course, client confidentiality is at the heart of my business practice. Even so, given the respectability of financial coaching, I've had to do my fair share of skulking around.

My most bizarre experience was a meeting at a client's home, arranged for when her husband was out. On hearing a knock on the door, my client jumped up like a frightened rabbit – she thought it might be her husband, who'd forgotten his keys. Thankfully, it wasn't – otherwise I'd have had to hide in the wardrobe.

Some women go to even greater lengths just to procure a secret credit card. Mind you, top marks for creativity must go to Sophie Kinsella's Becky Bloomwood in *Shopaholic & Sister*:

Dear Mrs. Brandon,

Thank you for your application for the High Status Golden Credit Card. We are glad to inform you that you have been successful. In answer to your questions, the card will be delivered to your home address and will resemble a credit card. It cannot be 'disguised as a cake' as you suggest. Nor can we provide a distraction outside as it arrives.

But if you've woven a Becky-sized web of deceit how can you start to come clean? Here are some ways of yielding up all your guilty secrets for inspection.

Five ways to own up about money problems:

1. Share the problem with someone, anyone, close to you. Say, 'I've got myself into a bit of a tricky situation and I need to tell you about it.' Then dive straight in there. If the words stick in your throat, try writing them a letter instead.

2. Contact a credit support helpline (see page 205) if you can't bring yourself to open up to a friend or family member. One phone call might be all that's needed to start the recovery process.

3. **Find** yourself a financial coach or therapist. They won't judge you and they'll offer lots of sensible, concrete guidance and support.

4. **Reveal** all by following the latest US trend and posting your financial secrets anonymously on internet 'debt blogs'. Some people find this gives them the accountability and discipline needed to help take control of the problem.

5. **Don't** try to go it alone or hide it from everyone, especially the closest person in your life who can be a source of support.

Jo's story

Jo was forty-six when a friend persuaded her to come to me for financial coaching. Her discomfort was apparent – this was the first time she'd talked to anyone about her financial chaos. And – one of more than 40 per cent of women who according to the Consumer Credit Counselling Service hide debt problems from their partners – Jo had even managed to keep Nigel, her husband of fifteen years, in the dark.

At our first session she produced the worksheets I'd asked her to complete. 'The most shocking part of filling them in,' she told me, 'was discovering I owe twenty-six thousand and five hundred pounds on credit and store cards. That's on top of my car loan. It's costing me eight hundred and sixty-two pounds and fifty pence a month – nearly a third of my income.'

Jo was horrified at the prospect of telling Nigel the truth about her finances; she felt sure he'd lose all respect for her. In my experience, women need a solution worked out before confronting their partners. Then at least they can soften the blow with a rescue plan.

Jo knew her revelation would put paid to Nigel's dreams of a swish new bathroom. And to their plans to visit his mother in Australia. She dreaded hitting him with this bombshell but realized she'd have to come clean. She was probably going to have to cash in their joint savings and maybe even release equity from their house to clear her debt. There was no way she could do that without Nigel's involvement. She'd also been ignoring the fact that the fixed rate deal on their mortgage had ended nine months ago. It was crazy not to switch to a more competitive rate and save nearly £140 a month, but this wasn't an option while her debt was still a secret.

With coaching, Jo was eventually able to own up to her husband – armed with all the possible solutions that we'd worked out. Their marriage survived the jolt and, afterwards, Jo felt as though a massive weight had been lifted from her. Of course, Nigel was disappointed that Jo had kept so much from him. But he'd admitted he'd been partly responsible – he'd turned a blind eye whenever he suspected Jo was spending beyond her means.

Nigel agreed to back the recovery plan one hundred per cent and, importantly, Jo and Nigel committed to have regular meetings in future where they would sit down, analyse their money situation and discuss their financial strategies together.

A problem shared . . .

As Jo found, and as we saw earlier in Monica's story, when you tell people you've got money problems it isn't like revealing you have bubonic plague. Friends worth their salt won't recoil in horror, they will want to help rather than judge you. Ironically, although we feel pathetic owning up to messy finances, we don't suddenly become a lesser being in the eyes of others. We may even become more 'human' in their eyes and, generally, they will be empathetic and caring.

Coming clean over a personal failing also makes it easier for others to do the same. It may not be a financial secret, but they will be more inclined to open up to you about some failing of their own if you've already disclosed one of your own mistakes to them. Mistakes' amnesty all round.

DO SOMETHING DIFFERENT: DIVULGE YOUR MONEY HABITS!

Put paid to being secretive about money. Get more financially intimate with your friends and loved ones. Share something about your finances that you've previously kept under wraps – the size of your mortgage perhaps, or the value of your house. Or confide in a friend about how much debt you've got, confess to having no pension arrangements or being unable to save. Share as much personal information as you wish – just disclose something that you would otherwise choose to keep to yourself.

The Sheconomics law **Share Financial Intimacies** is all about building trusting, honest relationships with others and with yourself in relation to money. This requires that you communicate in order to understand and come to terms with your own and your partner's money mindset. Agree to accept any differences between you and you'll be headed for financial bliss.

My Sheconomics Checklist
Law 6

How are you doing at sharing financial intimacies?   ✓

My partner and I have regular, relaxed money planning conversations	
I only buy presents for people I care about and spend only what I can afford	
I am open and honest with friends and family about my finances	
My partner and I have equal access to, and equal control over, our joint finances	
I never (OK, hardly ever) overindulge my children	
I can Do Something Different when it comes to sharing financial intimacies	

Chapter 8
Law 7: Know tomorrow comes

It is a truth universally acknowledged, that a single woman in possession of a good fortune must try very hard not to spend it all, and even put some into a pension.

(With apologies to Jane Austen)

As I cooed over my friend's newborn baby girl I wondered what sort of life little Jemima would have ahead of her. A statistic I'd heard recently said that one in four babies born in 2008 is likely to live for more than a hundred years. Wow, that's a long time, I thought, as she curled her tiny finger around mine. I almost wanted to ask her mum, 'Have you thought about her pension yet?' But I thought better of it.

The thing is, we're all living longer. And we women are outliving the men. A hundred years ago when the government introduced a state pension it made perfectly good sense. Because most people died long before they could get their hands on a pension book. Men died at an average age of forty-nine and women at fifty-three. Now, we're living well into our eighties and nineties. That means not only will more of us draw a pension. But we'll be drawing it for a long time, maybe even for thirty years or more.

Yet the future of the state pension in the UK is uncertain. And quite frankly it's deluded to think the State will provide for you when you retire. So, we've got to act quickly to make amends, or risk ending up like *Sex and the City*'s Carrie Bradshaw when she declared mournfully, 'I've spent forty thousand dollars on shoes and I have no place to live. I will literally be the old woman who lived in her shoes.'

Tomorrow does come and we can't ignore it. OK, pensions might seem very, very boring. But you can bet your bottom dollar that poverty's not very exciting either.

If you started work at, say, twenty-three, after going to university and hope to retire at the age of sixty, you will probably spend as many years in retirement as you spent working.

In this chapter we'll be giving you a run-down on how to not be a bag lady when you're older. We want you to see why you absolutely must start saving something – anything – for your retirement. We want you to know that when tomorrow comes, the money you put by today could add up to a pleasantly large pile. This is where you get the chance to make compound interest and the volatility of the stock market (we'll explain later) work in your favour.

You're going to learn to love your pension. To see it as a gorgeous, big cake that you'll start baking early, watch slowly rise and feast on in your dotage. You may be feeling comfortable now – perhaps you're on a reasonable salary, perhaps you can even boost your income with extra earnings – the trouble is, spending has a sneaky way of keeping pace with earning. And sometimes savings get sacrificed along the way. Or we forget that we might simply outlive our savings. But when your earning days are over, then what?

> *'I worry about not having any savings and constantly spending too much but I also don't want to change my lifestyle. I do want to look into saving money but it seems to be overwhelming and drains my energy just thinking about it.'*

This trainee Sheconomist's feelings aren't unusual. Here, we're going to help you balance your current needs against your future ones. Future needs tend to get drowned out when we're hedonistically indulging our current desires. We'll show you how it is possible to take care of both. And it's not just retirement we want you to plan for. Remember those goals you set in Chapter 5 (Sheconomics law 4: Have goals)? This is your chance to do some sums to see how you're going to turn those goals into reality.

You know those get-rich-quick schemes that you read about in the newspaper or hear discussed at dinner parties? Our mantra is 'get rich slowly'. Like yogic teachings, the best schemes are based on years of devoted practice, flexibility and with an eye on safety.

When you know tomorrow comes you will:

- Secure your future by doing the right thing today
- Map out the future the way you want it to be
- Be able to take care of things if they go wrong
- Enhance your freedom
- Expand your choices
- Live a full life, more balanced and with less stress

Act now

If you fear that reading all the inevitably rather boring stuff about savings, investments and pensions will make your head fall off, don't worry. Here are some things you can do right now. Today. Actions to make sure you get more than just a bus-pass when you enter your sixth decade.

Five Top Sheconomic Tips to Future-Proof Yourself

1. Save automatically

Divert an amount directly into savings every month. Make this a priority even if it's just fifty pounds. Start with something like a cash ISA (you can save up to £3,600 each tax year without getting taxed on the interest). Once you've built up enough of an emergency cushion, start to direct money monthly into a pension or investment plan. Those small savings can build up to massive sums in the long term. It pays to start early.

2. Join a pension scheme

If you get the chance to sign up to a company scheme, jump at it. Turning it down is like refusing free money because most companies will match your contributions and more. If you don't have that option, you'll need to make your own arrangements quickly – every year you put it off costs you dear. Just talk to a financial advisor if you're flummoxed.

3. Start paying attention to money

Financial freedom comes from being financially literate. Start to learn just a little bit about money today. Talk about it. Sign up to newsletters. Read the money pages in the weekend newspapers. Make it important to you. Hire yourself a coach, get yourself a mentor, or teach yourself – even enrol on the Open University's personal finance course.

4. Build your net worth (see page 142)

Look at ways to shrink your debt and boost your assets. Don't buy liabilities disguised as assets. Check your net worth year on year with the aim of increasing it annually.

5. Make money work hard for you

Wise up to what are the best returns on your savings or investments. Check them regularly. A 1 per cent difference in interest rates can add up to a huge sum with compounding (see page 176). Take advantage of tax efficient ISAs and pensions.

DO SOMETHING DIFFERENT: TAKE A LONG VIEW

Deep down we all know tomorrow comes. Why else do we do things every day to make our lives better in the future – such as cleaning our teeth so they won't all fall out. We don't say, 'I haven't got time to do that' or, 'Life's too short to brush my teeth'. Surprisingly though, lots of women use these types of excuses for not doing things with money that could guarantee them a comfortable future.

Think back to something you did years ago that didn't have an immediate pay-off but that now you're really glad you did.

Here are some examples from our trainee Sheconomists:

'I took extra Spanish lessons at school. Now my work involves travelling to South America. If I hadn't stuck with the Spanish I would never have landed such a fantastic job.'

'I've worn sunscreen on my face for as far back as I can remember. Now everyone marvels at my amazing, wrinkle-free skin.'

'Years ago I planted silver birch trees to shield an ugly view at the end of my garden. They were tiny at the time but now they are huge and give me beautiful shade and privacy.'

Imagine yourself when you're older saying:

'I started paying into a pension fund when I was in my twenties. It was the best thing I ever did. Now I have a wonderful life and do the things I love doing without ever having to worry about money.'

Beth's story

No one could accuse Beth of being backward in thinking forward. A client of mine for years, she's one of those women you hate but advisors love. She funded her pension and ISAs (PEPs and TESSAs in those days) to the maximum she was allowed from the age of twenty-four. She always earned a decent salary but, when most people would have ploughed it into living the high life, Beth made one important decision that has now changed her life.

Beth decided to take money seriously. Now, at the age of forty-three, she's got enough stashed away in savings, pensions and investments never to have to save another penny for the rest of her life. And the last decade hasn't been one of denial and deprivation either. She's still managed to have some wonderful holidays and weekends away, eat out at luxurious restaurants and to develop a taste for the best wines.

Beth was no different from you and me. She simply made a few different decisions. She took tenants in her flat so she could pay off her mortgage within fifteen years. She set up payments to go directly out of her account so she didn't notice her pay rises. She put a proportion of her bonuses from work into investments, keeping some back as a treat. She made money funding her employer's share incentive plans and selling them within her capital gains tax allowances at the right time. OK, at times she lost money. She wasn't immune to the various stock-market slumps. But she used those opportunities to invest more while prices were low. By making sure her investments were spread across different types of markets, she found that as one went down, there was often another going up. And she dripped money into her plans every month to keep her risk to a minimum.

At the age of forty-three Beth can practically afford to retire. She's not ready to yet but she has the freedom to choose different ways of working. She's considering taking a year off to travel. Or perhaps doing voluntary work abroad. We often think freedom comes from being able to buy whatever we want. But true freedom is when all the choices in the world are open to us.

And Beth's just like any of us. She's amazed that she's hit all her financial goals already. As far as she's concerned, if it was that easy, why aren't more women in her position? She doesn't feel she's done anything clever apart from getting sound advice at a young age. And acting on it.

If it's that easy, why don't we all do it?

There are a whole host of psychological reasons why we live in the present and ignore the future. Obviously, the present is here right now; we can get lots of lovely instant gratification and satisfy our whims without waiting. The future seems a world away, and delaying our pleasures isn't half as much fun.

Orphan Annie really summed up the way a lot of women feel when she sang, 'Tomorrow, tomorrow, I love you tomorrow. You're always a day away.' For some, tomorrow is far away to the point where it doesn't even exist. One trainee Sheconomist told us:

'I overspend a bit because I'm conscious that you can't take it with you. It would be nice to save up for a house – but I might die tomorrow.'

True, we might all die tomorrow. But, you know what? We probably won't. A conversation with another trainee Sheconomist summed up the issues for lots of women:

'Have you got a pension, Daniella?'

'No, I've been meaning to get one but haven't got round to it.'

'Why's that?'

'Because I've always been saving for something, first to go travelling, then for the flat and then the wedding. Since getting married I'm enjoying having some spending money for the first time in ages.'

Thinks then adds, *'Anyway, I wouldn't know where to go for one.'* A few seconds' silence then she says, *'And if I did I'd be scared of getting the wrong one.'*

Five Top Tips to Help You Plan For Your Future

1. Don't succumb to Peter Pan syndrome

It's too easy to believe, naïvely, that we're immune to the effects of ageing. To dream, instead, that Peter Pan will fly through the window and whisk us off to a world where no one ever has to grow up and think about nasty old pensions.

As daughters of Peter Pans we've witnessed denial of ageing at first hand: Simonne's dad is seventy-four, Karen's well into his eighties and neither acts their age – but we're hugely relieved their Peter Pan syndrome didn't extend to finance and they provided well for their futures.

Let's face it, some Peter Pans are terrific fun to be around, but you can have a fun-filled life and still make sure that down the line you'll be financially self-sufficient.

Women who suffer from Peter Pan syndrome glorify girliehood. They have the body of an adult and the financial mind of a little girl. They pursue sugar-coated short-term goals and all but stick their fingers in their ears if you mention the future. Or, like this trainee Sheconomist, they leave things to their dads to sort out.

'I get a kind of pulling in my gut whenever anyone talks about financial things. My dad's in his seventies and he's constantly trying to sit me down and explain things. But I just don't seem able to take it in. He's set up pensions and investments for me but I have no idea what they are.'

This attitude can come from being overprotected as a child. Overprotected children don't develop the skills to confront real life. For some women, bizarrely, this only applies to the financial side of their life. They can be completely savvy in all other areas but any mention of money brings out their helpless inner child.

On the other hand, the good news is that the Peter Pan syndrome affects more men than women. Not so good though if you're married to a financially immature Peter. In that case you might need to lead him by the hand through Chapter 7 (Share financial intimacies).

Are you a bit of a Peter Pan when it comes to money?

Do you:

- Keep promising yourself you'll start saving next year and then not get round to it
- Refuse to worry about the future because you know your earnings will keep going up

- Feel you've left it too late to start making provision for the future
- Think you deserve to live the way you want to now and stuff the future
- Believe that things will all sort themselves out somehow
- Feel life's too short to bother about the years to come and we should have fun now
- Have faith that the growth in property prices will see you through
- Think that Neverland is a real place

If you answered yes to more than three of the above, then you're at risk of permanently inhabiting financial Neverland. And you might need to do a bit more than wish on a star to rectify the situation.

What to do if this is you: Automate your savings. Find one thing that you can go without or cut back on. Put the cost of it into a savings account every month from now on. Pay yourself first before any other outgoings. Treat it as a priority, like your mortgage payments.

2. Avoid false sense of security syndrome

It's easy to get a false sense of financial security because you've ticked a few boxes. OK, maybe you're one of those rare people who's not in debt. Or maybe you've got a pension/got savings/own a property/have paid off your mortgage/have an ISA. So, you think, everything must be hunky-dory.

But when you ticked the box that said 'must get a pension' did you check out exactly what you were buying into? Do you know it's current value? If we asked you what income you're likely to get from it when you stop work, would you know? And, if you did know, are you sure it's enough to live on?

Paying off your mortgage seems to have become the holy grail of personal finance. There's even been a BBC TV programme called *Pay Off Your Mortgage in 2 Years* which seems to promote, among other things, the money-saving strategy of dining on cat food. That's fine. No, not eating cat food, that's disgusting. Paying off your mortgage is fine. But not if you do it at the expense of your old age provision. Because if you delay starting to save for retirement until the age of fifty, say, it will be outrageously expensive. You'll have missed out on the miraculous growth opportunities from compound interest. And there'll be fewer investments for you to choose from because you simply haven't got so long for them to grow.

So, we say invest for your future before you get sidetracked by other goals, *then* work at paying off your mortgage. We think it's a more sensible strategy. And eight out of ten financial advisors said they preferred it.

> **What to do if this is you:** Get a current value of any pensions, savings and investment plans and give some thought to what you want these plans to look like in five years.

3. Don't turn your back on employer benefits

Company pensions, where an employer contributes towards your pension, are almost always low on cost (to you) and high on returns. They really are too good to turn down. We can't say that loudly enough. **Company pensions really are too good to turn down.** Especially if you're one of the lucky few who still benefit from final salary schemes. By not joining, you're potentially waving goodbye to free money.

Private-sector employees can save up to £250 a month in a sharesave or save-as-you-earn (SAYE) scheme. This is a way of gradually saving towards buying shares with your employer, at a discount and tax efficiently. We love this type of scheme.

Find out if your employer runs a share incentive plan or will help with childcare cost in the form of childcare vouchers. Other benefits that can also crop up in employee benefits packages include death in service, critical illness cover, private medical insurance and long-term sick pay. Find out what your employer offers.

The very first company I (Simonne) worked for in the late eighties was an employee benefits consultancy. They advised other companies on benefits schemes. But ironically, most of their own staff had no idea about what schemes the company itself offered. I soon figured out all the benefits available and joined a twelve-month savings scheme to buy company shares at a discounted price.

Whereas I (Karen) had no idea what my first company offered. I didn't even know such schemes existed and, quite frankly, thought they had a bit of a cheek taking tax out of my wages. I've wised up a bit since then.

Simonne remembers explaining her employer's share scheme to a few colleagues and before long there was a rush of new applicants. Now she often asks human resources managers she meets how many staff take up their benefits package. The numbers are always depressingly low. It always distresses her that more people don't bother to find out how incredibly beneficial they can be.

What to do if this is you: Find out what your company offers. Join their pension scheme if you haven't already. Discuss the options with a professional if you need advice. Often your employer can arrange this for you for free. Just ask.

4. Don't sit at the back of the money class

Right, hands up. Who finds the world of pensions and investments easy to understand? None of us. That's fine. Many trainee Sheconomists find money achingly boring, one of them told us:

'I just see money as a means to an end. I'm not interested in saving or investing. I find it effortful to save money or make it grow on any scale. I know I should be more proactive and more in control of the bigger picture, but I buy myself treats on impulse in order to meet a frustrated immediate need.'

We have to stop being intimidated by the pension and investment world. It's easy to adopt a 'live for today' attitude, especially if you've had bad experiences of financial products in the past – or if you simply don't know what else to do with your money anyway.

But we have to stop doing nothing because we don't know what to do. To stop playing 'safe', for example by sticking to savings accounts because pensions and investments are too complex – or because we haven't got around to learning about risk and return.

Financial ignorance is unnecessary (you can always find out or get help) and expensive. For example, not understanding the difference between a fifteen-year and a twenty-five-year mortgage might cost you £70,000. Not knowing how to improve the returns on an investment could cost you *hundreds of thousands* of pounds (see Heather's story on page 292).

The zillions of financial products on the market mean we get overwhelmed by choice. But we'll let you into a little secret – most of them are all the same. Whatever you invest in falls into one or more of these four broad categories:

- **Cash:** money invested in banks or building societies that produce interest
- **Fixed interest**: where you loan money (to the government or a company) in return for a fixed interest
- **Shares:** you invest in someone else's business and hope they'll turn it into more money
- **Property:** buying either residential or commercial property to sell at a profit

If you can follow a few simple rules you can understand finance. Or you can find out where to go for help. Beware of taking well-intentioned, but often misguided, advice from just anyone, though. Talk instead to someone in-the-know. Someone you feel you can trust.

There's a well-known saying that goes, 'What you focus on gets bigger.' Be like Beth in the story earlier, and start to focus on your finances.

What to do if this is you: Sit down with someone who knows about money (maybe a friend, parent, colleague or even an adult child!) and ask them to explain something about finance that you hadn't previously understood. It's not a weakness to ask for advice. Beat off money-boredom by having a go at some of the Do Something Different exercises in this book.

5. Don't be scared off by risk

The words risk and safety mean different things to different people so make sure you know what they mean to you. The more you understand about finance, the more risk you'll feel comfortable taking.

Here are some comments on risk from a few trainee Sheconomists:

- *'Shares are too risky and not something I feel capable of understanding.'*
- *'I've heard too many horror stories about pensions. I'd prefer to keep my money in savings accounts.'*
- *'I'm happiest with property because at least it's tangible.'*
- *'I hate seeing my money go down in value.'*

While it's crucial for you to be comfortable with the level of risk you're taking, the biggest risk is to take no risk at all. And don't think that keeping your money under the mattress is the answer, because even that loses value with rises in inflation.

Generally speaking, investing in riskier products produces higher returns in the long run. And the longer you're prepared to hold on to an investment, the more risk you could plan to take. So savings accounts are fine for money needed in the short term. But share-based investments could be a better bet when you won't need the money for five to ten years or more (giving you time to recoup any losses). Having said that, stock markets can be incredibly volatile, so seek advice to help you decide what level of risk is acceptable to you.

You can cushion the effect of risk by not putting all your eggs in one basket. That means spreading between the different categories of investment we talked about on page 278: cash, fixed interest, shares and property. This way, you minimize your loses and increase your chances of one or more investments turning up trumps at any given time.

What to do if this is you: Work out how your money is divided between the four investment categories: cash, fixed interest, shares and property.

In the next section we're going deeper into savings, investments and pensions. If going there terrifies you, just keep this in mind. At the risk of gross oversimplification: **savings** are where you give your money to someone to look after; **investments** are where you put money into some other scheme and hope to turn it into more money and **pensions** are similar except you can't get your hands on the money until you're much, much older. But then it's usually worth much, much more. OK so far?

Savings

Savings are where you give your money to an organization (bank or building society) to take care of for you, and they pay you interest for that privilege.

Savings are low risk. When you put your money into a savings account you can be pretty sure of getting it all back, usually with interest. If you can wait a while before asking for it back (i.e. you don't need 'instant access') you may get a higher rate of interest. The best accounts currently offer an extra high rate of interest (up to 10 per cent AER) but they do ask you to commit to regular savings for twelve months.

You won't make a fortune having your money in savings. But savings are your financial security blanket. So if a big expense hits you, or you lose your job, you won't have to go into debt. The general rule of thumb here is to aim for a financial cushion of three times your monthly expenditure (or six months if you're self- employed) in readily accessible savings.

> *'I work all night I work all day and pay the bills I have to pay . . . And still there never seems to be a single penny left for me . . .'*

Abba's *Money Money Money* lyric summed up what a lot of women tell us. They simply can't save because they earn just enough to live on. Yet when I (Simonne) look at their spending there's always some way of cutting back painlessly. Perhaps they're overpaying on their insurances, are on the wrong mobile phone tariff or have a direct debit going out that they'd forgotten to cancel. These small amounts of money could be put away to earn more without them even noticing. Caroline's case was a typical one:

'I simply don't earn enough money to save and still have everything I want,' she said. Then she added, thoughtfully, *'I can't understand how people who earn less than me manage to save and appear to do everything.'*

Caroline is bewildered that there are women who are saving money and aren't wandering around in rags looking in need of a good meal. When we compared Caroline's outgoings with her friend Bernadette's, we noticed they both, as keen musicians, spent a lot on CDs. No problem there, music's their life-blood.

But Caroline bought hers on the high street while Bernadette bought hers online. On average Caroline was paying a third more. Reducing this cost alone recovered £30 a month that Caroline could put into savings. That's what Bernadette had been doing. Without making any lifestyle sacrifices. Caroline could also have simply upped the excess on her car insurance and saved a similar amount (see www.confused.com). Then, hey presto, that's £60 a month into her savings pot. With interest, she could have more than £750 at the end of a year without depriving herself at all.

DO SOMETHING DIFFERENT: TRICK YOURSELF INTO SAVING PAINLESSLY

Saving can be a chore, or something we never get around to doing.

Make it happen almost without you knowing it.

We've already mentioned automating your savings, so you treat yourself like paying any other bill and pay an amount from your salary into your savings account every month. And there are more:

- Overpay a bit on your mortgage every month.
- Pretend you didn't get a rise and divert the extra into savings.
- Transfer money into your savings account every time you save some money on a purchase, i.e. pay yourself the difference.
- Reinvest any interest or dividends from shares you receive.

These are all ways of saving money that won't hurt you – because you didn't 'know' you had the money in the first place.

Some savings accounts (especially ones that have been lingering for many years) offer a pitifully low rate of interest so it really is worth shopping around. Having £2,000 in an account that pays 1 per cent interest will give you just £20 interest. One that pays 5 per cent will give you £100. That's a lot extra for little effort.

Don't forget, the interest you earn on most savings is taxable. On many accounts tax at the basic rate will already have been deducted from the interest you receive. If you're a non-earner, and therefore a non taxpayer, you can fill in form R85 and have the interest paid gross, i.e. without the lender deducting the tax.

Whatever you do don't allow rescue fantasies to stop you from saving. Approximately one in two young people believe they'll inherit money to take care of them in the future. But parents are living longer and are more reluctant to give up a lifestyle they enjoy and, as a result of funding their longer lives, these silver spenders are leaving less money than before. Here's one trainee Sheconomist who was caught out by her parents' longevity:

'It never even occurred to me to finance my own old age. My parents were well off and when I was young I assumed I'd inherit their house when they died. It was a lovely big house and I thought the sale proceeds would see me through my retirement. In their latter years Mum

and Dad couldn't keep the house in a good state of repair and that affected the value of it. They both lived into their nineties. We had to sell their house to pay for them both to live in a residential home for the last seven years of their lives. There was virtually nothing left at the end. I'm nearly sixty now but if I live as long as my mother I've got another thirty-five years. To be honest, I just don't know how I'll manage and I dread even thinking about it.'

Five Tips for Saving Sheconomically:

- Compare the interest rates offered by different banks/building societies. Be careful with introductory offers that run only for a limited period or restricted withdrawals.
- Earn tax-free interest by saving in a cash ISA up to the amount allowed annually (currently £3,600 pounds per annum).
- If one of you is a non taxpayer, put joint savings into the non taxpayer's name and fill in form R85 to receive interest without tax deducted.
- If one of you pays basic rate tax and the other a higher rate, consider holding more savings in the name of the one who pays less tax.
- Instead of earning interest on your savings, some mortgages allow you to set up a linked savings account (often called an offset account) and have the interest on your mortgage reduced in line with what your savings would earn.

What's the difference between AER and APR?

Annual Equivalent Rate (AER) is used for savings accounts. It allows you to compare products that pay annual interest with ones that pay monthly on a like-for-like basis. If AERs are the same, the interest you'll receive will be identical whether it's paid monthly or annually. You're always looking for the highest AER not APR when it comes to savings accounts.

Annual Percentage Rate (APR) is used more for credit such as loans, mortgages, credit cards and overdrafts. It allows you to compare credit products by taking account of fees as well as the interest rate. Always look for the lowest APR when it comes to borrowing money.

Investments

Investments are ways of building up money in a way that's usually riskier and less accessible than standard savings accounts. Unlike savings, investments don't necessarily guarantee you'll get back what you put in. But they have greater potential for your money to grow.

Some investments provide growth (so that the original amount you invest grows – or at least that's the idea), others provide you with an income (regular payouts) and the rest offer income with some prospect of growth as well. So it depends on what goal you're planning as to what would be best for you.

There are tons of investment products available. It seems confusing but here are just five main points to take into consideration when choosing:

1. How much money you want to invest
Smaller amounts aren't suitable for some investments and you're sometimes restricted on the amount you can invest.

2. Your objectives
Be clear about whether you need an income from the money invested or whether you'd rather increase the chances of the money growing.

3. How long you're prepared to tie your money up for
Share prices go up and down so, if you're investing in these, you need to know that you can ride out the highs and lows. There's nothing worse than having to sell when the value of a shareholding or fund is at a low point.

4. The amount of risk you're prepared to take
Generally, risk and return are inversely related. The more you're prepared to risk, the more you stand to make over the long-term. Or lose.

5. Your tax position

You may need to seek advice as to which products are the most tax-efficient for you.

DO SOMETHING DIFFERENT: PLAY FTSE WITH YOUR FRIENDS!

Ever taken part in a sweepstake where you pick a horse's name out of a hat and all chip in to see who wins a big race like the Grand National?

Why not have a share sweepstake with your friends? You don't even have to put money in. Just each pick a company from the FTSE 100.

Don't worry if you don't understand all the numbers. Just choose one that appeals to you.

Look at the price on the London Stock Exchange website on the day you start. Then have a competition to see whose company increases its share value the most over the course of a month.

It's just for fun but it'll get you into the habit of watching how share prices change over time. And if you do pick one whose share price trebles in a month, you might start wondering 'What if I'd bought a hundred of those last month?'

Eight Great Sheconomist Investment Tips

- **Don't put all your eggs in one basket** Take a long-term view and spread your money between different investment markets. That way you'll benefit when a drop in the value of one asset is offset by the rise in value of another.

- **If your stock market based investment** has a fixed maturity date, gradually arrange for your investments to be transferred into more cautious funds as maturity approaches. If it's open-ended, consider your money committed for at least five years but preferably until such time as it's shown a good return (which could take longer).

- **Maximize your returns** by investing in tax-efficient plans like a stocks and shares ISA where no tax is paid on gains you make and interest is tax-free.

- **Check the charges** Low charges aren't always best but reducing charges has the same effect as increasing performance. So you need to weigh this up.

- **Look at publications** like *Money Management* as well as websites that offer free information on funds, so you don't just go for names that you know.

- **Don't let the tax-tail wag the dog** In other words, don't invest in something just because it's tax-efficient. For example, although you can invest £25 a month tax free in friendly society bonds, the high charges and inflexibility often outweigh the tax advantages.

- **Don't focus on avoiding losses but on making gains** Never be scared to sell poorly performing endowments or funds. Warren Buffett, a successful stock market investor, says we should, 'attempt to be fearful when others are greedy, and to be greedy only when others are fearful'.

- **Don't invest all in one go** With share-based investments it's better to drip money in on a monthly basis, rather than all at once at one price. That way you're not crossing your fingers, saying to yourself, 'I hope today's a good day to invest.' Instead, there's more chance you'll catch some when prices are low.

Equities – another name for stocks and shares

Don't be fooled by all the investment jargon. An equity is just another name for stocks and shares. And the words 'stocks' and 'shares' are interchangeable, too. They all mean the same thing – owning a stake in someone else's business. The stock market price of shares can go up and down. Share values are affected not only by how the company itself is doing but also by the overall level of confidence in the economy at home, and the international economic climate.

You can either buy shares in a company direct or invest in a fund. This spreads your risk by buying shares in several different companies. Funds are usually managed by a fund manager who decides which companies to invest in, when to buy stock and when to sell.

The other alternative is to invest in a fund that simply tracks a stock market index (known as an index, or tracker, or passively managed fund). For example, a tracker fund usually tracks the FTSE 100 index or FTSE All-Share index in the UK, the American S&P 500 or the German DAX. By investing in tracker funds you avoid the risk of a fund manager doing a lousy job.

Most fund managers don't do as well as the Index that they're tracking. Burton Malkiel, author of *A Random Walk Down Wall Street*, says that a blindfolded chimp throwing darts could pick stocks as well as the 'experts'. So why not go with an index or tracker fund and have the job done by a computer – and pay much lower fees. Historically, tracker funds do better than actively managed funds when markets rise, but don't do as well in challenging market conditions.

You can also invest in an equity fund through an ISA with up to £7,200 per tax year (£3,600 if you've already put £3,600 into a Cash ISA – these are based on the 2008/09 limit). Then you don't have to pay tax on money you make in the fund. Also higher rate taxpayers don't have to pay extra income tax on dividends (the profits paid out to shareholders).

You can invest in corporate bond funds through an equity ISA too. This is a lower risk alternative to investing in stocks and shares. Corporate bonds are like IOUs from companies, where they borrow money from you and, in exchange, promise to pay a regular rate of interest over a fixed period. They're suited to the more cautious investor or for the low risk part of a balanced range of investments.

Heather's story

When Heather was aged twenty-five her grandfather died and left her a decent-sized inheritance. She took her parent's advice and invested £25,000 of it in an investment bond. The idea was that it would grow and provide for her long-term future. She was able to withdraw the funds after ten years but she kept on rolling the investment forward while she didn't need the money.

Heather came to see me just after she'd turned fifty and brought along the statement relating to her investment. 'It's now worth nearly £84,000,' she exclaimed excitedly, before telling me of her dream to take early retirement.

In fact, Heather's investment had returned about 5 per cent a year growth. She seemed happy with that, but I was less than impressed. A quick mental calculation told me it could have been double.

Even if her investment had generated returns of 7 per cent a year (that's pretty realistic and not dramatically high) she would have ended up with £135,686 – that's £51,036 more, the equivalent of having saved an extra £85 a month every month for those twenty-five years.

At 8 per cent she'd have ended up with £171,212 – that's £86,562 more – which she'd otherwise have had to save £145 every month to achieve.

In the twenty-five years leading up to December 2007, shares have actually increased by 8.8 per cent a year on average. And that's after inflation. So even 12 per cent a year wouldn't have been an unrealistic expectation for Heather's investment. I didn't like to mention to her that this would have turned her £84,000 into an astonishing £425,000!

The effect of improving investment returns (or reducing charges, which can produce similar effects) is more dramatic than people realize.

It wasn't so much making the wrong investment decision twenty-five years before, but more the failure to review it, that was Heather's downfall. She had an old-style investment policy. It was expensive in terms of charges and the fund she was invested in was producing pretty mediocre returns. Even if she'd switched to another fund within the same plan with better prospects for growth, or taken a bit more investment risk perhaps, she'd have had a lot more to play with by now.

In Heather's case it meant the difference between having to continue to work for another five years and retiring, comfortably, today.

DO SOMETHING DIFFERENT: GO CLUBBING WITH YOUR MATES

If you fancy having a dabble in the stock market but (a) you don't want to go it alone and (b) you don't want to put in too much money, then it's easier and more fun to get together with some friends and invest.

Each person agrees to put £25 a month into the investment club funds. If there are ten of you that gives you £250 a month to invest.

Thousands of women invest in this way. They have regular social meetings and help each other to make money. Have a look at www.proshareclubs.co.uk

The other 'investments' we make

There's a bit of a conspiracy around. It concerns taking any extortionately priced, luxury purchase and boldly declaring it an investment. This gives wanton spending on extravagant purchases a mask of respectability. One fashionista was heard declaring on the radio that she 'invests' in a designer handbag every season. This isn't really investing. It's deluded self-justification of the sort indulged in by author Sophie Kinsella's shopaholic, Becky Bloomwood:

'A simple sleeveless dress from Whistles, the highest of Jimmy Choos, a pair of stunning, uncut amethyst earrings . . . This is investment shopping. The biggest investment of my life.'

On the other hand, some people invest seriously in art, wine or antiques. On the plus side, these investments mean you may have the pleasure of looking at them every day. The downside is that the fickleness of markets makes their future growth uncertain. You could end up needing to sell something that nobody wants to buy. So don't make them your only safeguard for the future. And, if you choose to invest in this way, just make sure you love the things you've put your money into. At least if they don't materialize into capital you'll have had years of pleasure from them – or end up being a very poor but very drunk vintage wine collector.

Tip
Use the Rule of 72 to work out when your money will double

If you have money to invest and your aim is to double it, use this trick to work out how long that will take.

Take the number 72 and divide it by the annual investment return or interest rate you're getting.

So, for example, if the return is 10 per cent a year, it would take 7.2 years to double the money. At 6 per cent a year, it would take 12 years. At 8 per cent a year, it would take 9 years. And so on.

Investing in property
The prospect of a quarter of a century of mortgage repayments and endless weekends wandering around

Homebase haven't been enough to deter millions of people from becoming homeowners. Property is what we Brits love to invest in. In the UK, buying a home is one big step on the ladder to social acceptability and success. Although we frown on debt we love mortgages and no one is ever ashamed to own up to having one. Strange really.

But then buying your own home is a great first investment. Always think of it as a medium- to long-term investment. In other words, consider yourself committed for at least five years. It's not something to go into lightly – or jointly with someone you haven't known long or aren't even sure you get along with.

House prices tend to rise but they can also go down. As with stocks and shares, so long as you can ride it out and wait for the right time to sell, you should be fine. Also, remember, a mortgage is secured against your home. You must keep up the mortgage payments, otherwise your home could be repossessed and you may lose the money you put into it.

Mortgages

There are two factors to consider when choosing a mortgage: the type of interest deal on the loan and the method of repaying it.

The main types of interest deals are:

A **discounted** or **tracker-rate mortgage** (where the interest rate usually rises at the end of a set period). A mortgage that **tracks** the bank base rate is guaranteed to rise and fall in line with changes in the rate of interest set by the Bank of England. **Discounted** deals don't always pass on falls in rates (although they sure as hell pass on increases). So, of the two, assuming like-for-like starting rates, tracker deals are usually best. Choose this if you think that interest rates will go down and accept the risk that they may go up.

A **fixed rate mortgage** where the interest rate doesn't change but gives you the certainty of knowing what your mortgage payments will be for a set period of time.

A **standard variable rate mortgage** (where the interest can rise or fall in future) at a rate determined by the lender. Most mortgage deals revert to this loan type once any set period is up. This is usually the most expensive option, so only stay on this type of loan if you need flexibility.

The options for paying back the loan are:
repayment, **interest-only** or a **combination of the two**.

With a **repayment mortgage** your monthly payments gradually pay off the whole loan by the end of the agreed mortgage term, as well as the interest.

With an **interest-only mortgage** your monthly payments
are cheaper. But they cover only the interest on the loan,
not the money borrowed. So at the end of the term you
still owe the initial amount loaned and have to find a way of
paying that off all in one go. You'll need to make separate
payments into an investment scheme to build up enough
capital to pay off the loan by the end of the term (if not
before) – but if the investments don't grow as well as you'd
hoped, you may come unstuck. This happened with a lot
of endowment policies sold in the eighties and nineties. So
if you go down this route, choose your investments
carefully and make sure you know what you're going into.

Remember: you can have a mortgage that's made up of
different types – part repayment, part interest-only, part
fixed, part variable interest.

Here are our top Sheconomist tips on buying your own home

- **Shop around** Get the best mortgage deal you can. On a
  £150,000 mortgage a 1 per cent interest rate saving
  could save you as much as £30,000 over twenty-five
  years.

- **Club together** Consider buying with a friend or friends
  to get onto the property ladder. That's how I (Simonne)
  bought my first property.

- **Watch for fees and charges** Arrangement fees can be as much as £2,500. Brokers may suggest adding such charges to your mortgage loan but over twenty-five years that £2,500 costs you nearer £5,000.

- **Avoid a Mortgage Indemnity Premium (MIP)** This covers the lender against any loss on selling the property if you default on the mortgage. Some lenders insist on it if you are borrowing a high proportion of the value of the property, e.g. 90 per cent or more – and they like to add it to your mortgage.

- **Account for all the costs when buying** As well as the deposit you'll pay solicitor's fees, lender's valuation fee, survey fee, stamp duty, mortgage arrangement fee, MIP (possibly), even the cost of mortgage advice as well as removals and . . . And that's before you've put a stick of furniture into the place.

- **Don't buy home insurance from your mortgage lender** They are usually the most expensive. And avoid other unnecessary or overly expensive insurance policies they try to flog you. Be especially wary of payment protection insurance (PPI). This is expensive and many people find they can't claim on it.

- **Check whether there will be penalties** if you pay off part or all of the mortgage early.

- **Be ready to change** You don't have to stick to one lender for the whole mortgage term. Review the mortgage every few years and see if you'd get a better deal by switching.

- **Keep the end in mind** Don't shift the end date of your mortgage every time you move. Many people start with a twenty-five-year loan, maybe taking them to age fifty-five. They then move after six years and opt for twenty-five years again, shifting the end age to sixty-one, and then again a few years later. Try to reduce the term each time you move.

Pensions

Pensions are really just another kind of tax-efficient wrapper you put around a long-term investment. There's nothing mysterious about a pension; it's basically a pot of money that you build up which you can't dip into before you reach a certain age. That age is currently fifty (fifty-five from 2010) but the younger you are when you take money from your pension, the more you'll need to have invested.

When you draw on the pension, some of it becomes available as cash. Usually that's 25 per cent of the total fund. And it comes as a tax-free lump sum. The rest gets invested to give you an annual income until you die (known as an annuity). You don't even have to actually retire to draw on a pension; you can carry on working if you wish.

As an incentive for saving towards retirement, the government credits you with tax relief on money you pay into a pension (within set limits). This means that every £80 you pay in gets topped-up to £100. Higher-rate taxpayers only have to pay £60 for that same £100 investment which immediately gives them 66 per cent more in their pension plan. Money invested in a pension grows tax efficiently too, so you can make as much money as you like within the plan without having to pay any tax on the gains.

'I'm terrified of being alone. I have a feeling that Barry will probably die before me and I want to be financially secure. I always thought it would be great to understand more about money. I want to learn more, take control and make best use of what I have.'

Many of us think of retirement as a time when we'll finally get rewarded for all the effort we put in during our working life. Charming images of smiling, elderly couples cycling through the countryside looking financially smug – probably off to buy another condominium on Miami beach (and one for the children) – sell us the utopian dream of future freedom.

But for many women even a bike could be a luxury item when they hit retirement age because lots of us won't have anything like the same amount of disposable income in retirement that we had during our working lives. Fewer than half of all women who reach state pension age currently get a full basic state pension. That's compared to over 80 per cent of men.

And if you do end up being one of the 'lucky' ones who gets a state pension, you're not exactly in for a life of luxury – think more repeats of *Miami Vice* on the telly than a condo on Miami beach. The basic State pension at the moment is only £90.70 (as at April 2008) a week. That's £30 less than the amount the government reckons we need to live on in a week. A hefty portion, if not all, of that £90 will go on utility bills and food.

You may qualify for some additional state pension based on your earnings. This is called the State Second Pension – the replacement for SERPS. But even then, the extra isn't a huge amount and it won't provide the quality of life to which you'd like to become accustomed. Plus it isn't a funded scheme, which means that there's no guarantee it'll be there in the future.

In the UK, state pensions only kick in once you've reached the age of sixty-five, or a little earlier if you're a woman born before 1955. And the pension age is increasing from sixty-five to sixty-eight between 2024 and 2046, so you really must make savings elsewhere if you plan to retire any earlier.

The main types of pensions schemes include

Final Salary company pension Your pension at retirement age is based on your income when you stop working for the employer and the number of years you've been in the scheme. The pension is paid from retirement age for the rest of your life. It also increases each year in line with minimum standards, so it's definitely not one to be sniffed at.

Money Purchase company pension A kind of savings plan. The amount of pension you get depends on the amount paid in, how well it all grows, the charges deducted and the rate at which you can swap your pension fund for an income in retirement.

Additional Voluntary Contributions (AVCs) Top-up contributions you can make if you're in a company pension scheme. Contributions qualify for tax relief at your highest rate and operate like a money purchase scheme. AVC schemes are run by your employer, whereas free standing (FS)AVC schemes are like private versions of an AVC and can be set up independently of your employer. AVCs tend to cost less than FSAVCs but you usually have fewer investment choices.

Personal Pensions (including Stakeholder schemes) Available from insurance and investment companies. These work like a money purchase pension. Just about anyone can buy one and they're especially suitable for the self-employed or if your employer doesn't run a company scheme. Stakeholder pensions are similar to personal pension plans but have low charges and can be more flexible than traditional personal pensions.

Self Invested Personal Pensions (SIPPs) A personal pension plan where you get to make your own decisions about how to invest the retirement pot. It's like a DIY version of a pension. You have more freedom and choice over how the funds are invested but some can be expensive.

Group Personal Pensions This is the same as a personal pension but where your employer offers the scheme to their staff and may offer lower charges than personal pensions arranged by yourself.

We're all living longer and healthier lives. Your pension, as one trainee Sheconomist coined it is, 'like a gift to your future self'. So, just imagine, your retirement could last as long as thirty or forty years. It really is time to think seriously about how you're going to finance those golden years. The longer you leave it, the harder it'll be.

According to a report by Prudential, more than half of all non-retired UK adults have no private or company pension arrangements. And of those that do, many seriously underestimate how much they need to pay in if they're not to be left financially challenged on retirement.

But the messages here aren't all doom-laden. There are ways of putting money away and getting about five times more back at retirement. Company pensions are a good example. With tax relief, employer's contribution and compound interest it really is madness not to jump (while you're still young enough to jump) on the pension bandwagon.

The secret is to get cracking as soon as you possibly can, and pay in a percentage of your income, so that your contributions automatically keep pace with your earnings. A very rough rule of thumb, if you're taking out a pension for the first time, is to start with contributions based on half your age. So a thirty year old needs to pay 15 per cent of their income into their pension pot, but if they started at forty they'd need to make it 20 per cent.

Look at the example below. It illustrates the pension income that you could expect from paying in £240 a month (topped up by the government to £300 a month) at different starting ages.

Age at start	Projected pension, in today's terms, at 65
25	£1,205 per month
35	£745 per month
45	£416 per month
55	£173 per month

Your pension cake

Remember we said you'd come to think of your pension as a big, gorgeous cake that you're baking to have in the future. You'll only have paid for two slices of that cake yourself. The rest will be paid for by others, but you get the whole cake to yourself. How fabulous is that?

Sue's cake

Let's take the case of Sue. Sue's just started working for an IT company and earns £48,000 a year. As part of her package her employer will pay into a pension scheme of her choosing. They'll match her contributions of £300 a month. As a higher-rate taxpayer, it cost Sue just £180 a month for £300 to be invested (nicely topped up by the government's tax relief of £120 a month). If she stays in the scheme until she's sixty-five (she's thirty-five now) and the contributions stay the same all the way through, at sixty-five she'll have a retirement pot of £358,400.

Out of this only 18 per cent will have come from Sue herself. The rest comes from her employer, tax relief from the government and growth on the money invested.

Looking ahead, Sue retires at sixty-five with total fund value of £358,400 of which:

- £64,800 was paid in by Sue in contributions each month (18 per cent)
- £108,000 was paid by the employer (30 per cent)
- £43,200 is tax relief (12 per cent)
- £142,400 is compound interest Sue got on the pension money invested (40 per cent)

Here's Sue's pension cake. It's huge and very satisfying. And, to get all this, all she had to do was pay in the equivalent of two slices from the age of thirty-five until she retired at sixty-five.

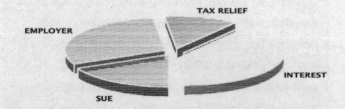

*The cake that's too good to turn down. **Sue's pension is made up of lots of contributions. She only paid for a couple of slices but she gets the whole cake.***

Recipe for a great big pension cake

Step 1: Pre-heat the oven

In other words, start as early as you can. The longer you put it off the less your chance of getting the whole gorgeous cake. And who really wants just a measly slice? So get cracking and cook your cake long and slow.

Step 2: Get all the ingredients together

Find out what you've already got. Get a forecast of your state pension and age of retirement from the Pensions Service at www.thepensionservice.gov.uk.

Dig out any other pensions and get an estimate of income from them in today's terms. Or get a current fund value and plug this information (plus future contributions if appropriate) into an online calculator such as www.pensioncalculator.org.uk/

If you're an active member of a company pension scheme, ask your employer for a forecast of your pension, in today's terms, at the scheme's normal retirement age.

Look at other sources of retirement income (e.g. from downsizing your home or selling a business) and get a guestimate of what income to expect from this. Dividing the total provided by these other sources by twenty-five will give you a rough estimate of the annual income it could provide.

Step 3: Top up the missing ingredients

In other words, see what the shortfall is between what you've got and what you'll need in retirement.

Look at your expenses and figure out what will change once you stop work. Deduct your expenses from the annual income you calculated at Step 2. Or, as a rule of thumb, assume it'll be seventy-five per cent of your current income if you're living well now. Is there a shortfall between your income needs when you retire and what your income is likely to be at that time?

Use an online pension calculator such as www.pensioncalculator.org.uk/ to estimate how much extra money you'd need to save in order to reach the target income. Enlist the help of a finance professional if this feels a little too complicated.

Step 4: Keep an eye on the cake while it's baking

Don't just leave it to cook and forget about it. Keep it under review. Look at how your investment is performing and make sure it's still competitive. You can turn up the heat by switching providers or funds if you wish.

Review your pension contributions regularly. Make sure you're on track for enough to live on when you retire. And don't forget – always ask for projections in today's terms.

Maia's story

'I haven't got the foggiest idea where my money's going,' was Maia's response when I asked her about her relationship with money. Maia had come to see me to learn how to make the most of her finance.

While going through her paperwork, we came across an old Scottish Widows policy. Then we found a nine-year-old statement relating to the same plan. It turned out there was £22,000 in this pension policy. There were no more recent statements because Maia had moved address years ago and hadn't notified the company.

When we did some investigating, we discovered this plan was now worth more than £32,000. Maia had been contracted out of SERPS/S2P and Scottish Widows had been collecting payments from her national insurance contributions that she wasn't even aware of.

Although it was good to come across this policy, it turned out to be rather a plodding fund that wasn't really going anywhere and it was also quite expensive. Maia took advice and transferred it to a better scheme that would provide her with a good-sized cake upon her retirement.

I (Simonne) regularly come across women who don't know what plans they have or what their plans are worth. Some don't have any paperwork, others may do but they don't understand it. As a result lots of policies go unclaimed and women miss out on money that's rightly theirs.

What to do if this is you: Think back to the last couple of times you moved house. Did you notify absolutely everyone of your new address? Have you mislaid the paperwork on the account or plan? Don't write it off, your money's still out there somewhere. Perhaps you have some distant memory of pension you once held with a previous employer. Perhaps you vaguely recall starting an investment plan or savings account, once. Somewhere. It can be tracked down.

There are websites designed for this very purpose. One is www.mylostaccount.org.uk which guides you through the process of tracing lost savings accounts. And the government's pensions website www.thepensionservice.gov.uk helpfully has a section specifically for lost pensions. Or, if you're time poor, you can pay to have lost life policies, pensions, savings or investments tracked down for you at www.uar.co.uk

I (Simonne) have a friend who's worked as a civil servant for years. Years ago she let slip to me that she hadn't joined the pension scheme. I was an independent financial advisor at the time and came across this quite a lot with my clients. Their defence was either: (a) they couldn't afford it, or (b) they didn't think they'd be in the job for long, or (c) they hadn't got around to filling out the paperwork.

In my friend's case it was (a). She was always strapped for cash. I had to find a tactful way of explaining why she couldn't afford not to join – especially as it was a final salary scheme. After several attempted discussions at which she rapidly changed the subject, I resorted to the shock factor: I worked out the cost of her reluctance – that she'd effectively waved goodbye to £40,000. That was many years ago and in the meantime her earnings have increased significantly so, in today's terms she'd have lost more like £60,000. I'm glad to say that (probably to stop me nagging) she did, in fact, join the scheme and has never regretted it.

Eight facts women should know about retirement planning

1. We're still, on average, earning less than men. We must save a bigger proportion of our income to get the same retirement pot as men.

2. Our earning power often takes a hit if we have children or take on other caring responsibilities. This affects the size of our pension, too.

3. We tend to live longer than men. We need to save more than men to secure our financial future because our pension has to last us longer.

4. We tend to invest less aggressively than men. We might get poorer returns and have to invest more to end up with the same pot in retirement.

5. Women tend to lose more money than men following a divorce.

6. We're more likely than men to spend our disposable income on our children.

7. Most working women (more than four million in the UK) don't save enough for retirement. The same number again are not saving at all.

8. Most of us miss out on a full state pension. Either we haven't earned enough or haven't built up enough years of contributions.

DO SOMETHING DIFFERENT: LIVE ON THE STATE PENSION FOR A WEEK EXPERIMENT

A couple's state pension and means-tested pension credit is £189.35 a week. For a single pensioner (as of April 2008) it's just £124.05. Think you could live on that? Why not try it for just one week to get a taste of what it could be like.

If you have alternative pension arrangements find out what your weekly retirement income would be in today's terms. And try living on that for a week to see if it really is adequate.

Assuming you'll own a property by the time your retire, with no rent to pay, subtract the cost of your weekly bills from your pension. What's left is your disposable income. That's what you can spend on food and entertainment. (Leaving aside the odd emergency and presents for the grandchildren.)

When they lived by this experiment, journalist, Antonia, and her husband were left with £68 a week. They were horrified that even the local bingo dive charges £10 admission. Antonia nearly blew the food budget on a couple of bottles of wine and her husband threatened divorce if she fed him 'another plate of bloody lentils'.

At the end of the experiment they were convinced that an overflowing private pension pot is the key to a happy, lentil-free retirement. The bingo they could live without – but not the odd steak and glass of wine.

Not everyone wants a pension

Depending on your circumstances and plans for the future
– perhaps you plan to live abroad or have a nest-egg
already – you may need, or want, to keep your
investments flexible. You could, for example, make regular
payments into a stocks and shares ISA instead of a
pension (for a basic-rate taxpayer, the tax benefits would
be roughly equivalent) which would allow more freedom to
do whatever you wished with any other investments.

Although pensions are usually the most tax-efficient way of
providing retirement income (particularly for higher-rate
taxpayers), your retirement cake could be concocted from
a mixture of pensions, equity ISAs, cash and other
investments.

Equity ISAs are a popular alternative to pensions, especially
to basic-rate taxpayers. Really they're just as tax efficient
and more flexible. Although you don't get tax relief on your
ISA contributions (as you would with a pension), they can
provide a tax-free income. ISAs also give you the freedom
to choose how you use the money. You may wish to pay
off a mortgage, help towards the cost of education for the
children or supplement your income when you stop work.

You can invest £7,200 a year in equity ISAs (based on
2008/09 figures) and any more than this can be invested
in shares. But remember, gains from those may be subject

to capital gains tax and dividends/income are taxable too.
But you do have the flexibility and control that you have
with ISAs that pensions simply don't offer.

Providing protection for you and your family
Insurance. What a pain. But sometimes you just have to
have it. Life insurance is pretty crucial because it makes
sure that your dependents would have enough to live on if
you died – and vice versa. Amazingly though, some
women pay out for life insurance when they don't have
any dependents or jointly hold any debt. There's no point.

Then there are all those other insurances: house contents,
critical illness, health, pet insurance, travel insurance,
wedding insurance, nail extension insurance (don't laugh,
it's probably only a matter of time). These types of
insurance are all optional; you're not obliged to have them.
All you have to insure, by law, is your car and the property
you live in, if you have a mortgage on it.

As a rule of thumb, aside from insurance you have to have
by law or contract, only insure against losses you can't
cover yourself.

So it's worth weighing up the likelihood of the risk against
the cost. Are you, for example, paying extra for rabies
protection on your dog's insurance even though she's so
old she hardly ventures outside the back door? I (Karen)

was recently sold a camera by a young man who insisted it was the most reliable model on the market. The store had never had one returned or reported faulty, he claimed. As I paid for it he tried to convince me I needed extended warranty insurance. I reminded him of his sales pitch and told him 'no thank you'. I prefer to put the money towards a new model in three years' time.

Top Sheconomist Tips For Providing Protection For You And Your Family

- **Don't spend more than you need to** Insurance is one of those things where you don't always get what you pay for. More expensive isn't necessarily better. Compare like for like and take the cheapest.

- **You may need less life insurance** if you have a pension or employer scheme that pays out in the event of death.

- **Don't be bullied into taking out insurances** against risks that don't bother you – like critical illness or mortgage/loan payment protection.

- **Buy insurance through a discount broker** This way you'll pay lower premiums because you'll save the commission. You will have to make your own decisions about the insurer and type of insurance though. Have a look at www.moneyworld-ifa.co.uk or www.cavendishonline.co.uk for quotes.

- **Set up a trust for life insurance** to be paid outside of your estate. This will save inheritance tax and there won't be the delay of waiting for probate to be settled.

- **Have an up-to-date will** Especially if you have children. You should stipulate who'll look after them if you die. Otherwise it'll be left to the State to decide. Even if you're single or childless a will is important. Without one your assets will be divvied up according to the laws of intestacy.

- **Appoint an enduring power of attorney** Someone who'll look after your financial affairs if, say, you had a sudden accident that left you in a coma.

- **Check your insurance polices once a year** to make sure they still reflect your circumstances. And to check they're still competitively priced.

DO SOMETHING DIFFERENT: WRITE TO YOURSELF IN THE FUTURE

Write a letter to your future self. In it make a promise to your future self that you have taken care of her and acted with her interests in mind.

Pledge that you haven't squandered everything short-term, or you'll have some explaining to do to your future self.

List what you have done to protect yourself against future hardship as well as what you intend to do.

Prove to your future self that you know tomorrow comes. Then read the letter when it does come. You can even create the letter on www.futureme.org and set a date in the future when the letter will be emailed to you!

My Sheconomics Checklist

Law 7

Do you know tomorrow comes?   ✓

I save automatically each month	
I have arrangements in place for my retirement	
I regularly monitor the returns my savings and investments are earning	
I balance investment risk by choosing different financial products	
I am not relying on anyone but myself for my future financial security	
I'm willing to Do Something Different when it comes to planning for my future	

Chapter 9
A day in the life of . . . A top Sheconomist

7.00 a.m. Alarm goes off, I slept like a log! Probably because Josh and I had a lovely chat last night about the holiday flat and our future together. Now we're in tune with each other's money mindsets these heart-to-hearts are so much easier.

> Law 6:
> Share financial intimacies

7.15 a.m. Do some yoga before my shower – great for clearing my head before the day starts.

7.45 a.m. Load up the juicer with carrots and apples bought from the market at end of play yesterday; knock-down price and much healthier and tastier than shop-bought juice. Carrying cash now means I can grab these bargains.

> Law 3:
> Spend with power

8.00 a.m. Kept the financial section of the weekend newspaper and read it over breakfast. Read an interview in it

> Law 1:
> Take emotional control

about a woman who built up a multi-million pound business after starting off making soaps from home. She had to approach twelve banks before she could get backing, but she never gave up. Gets me thinking again about my dream to run my own design business and having the will to make it happen.

> Law 2:
> Go beyond beliefs

8.20 a.m. The post arrives. Official-looking envelopes don't scare me any more and I open the credit card statement immediately. Do a quick scan of the entries. Feel relieved I set up a direct debit to clear it monthly. File it into my folder.

> Law 1:
> Take emotional control

8.30 a.m. Pack the hummus I made last night into my bag, plus some pita breads from the freezer and the rest of the fruit from yesterday's market haul and fill up my water bottle from the tap. Cherie picks me up; it's her turn to drive this week since we started car-sharing to work.

> Law 3:
> Spend with power

9.00 a.m. At work I get letter from human resources to confirm the

> Law 7:
> Know tomorrow comes

additional voluntary contributions I'm
making for my pension. Check online
what my pension fund will be in today's
terms when I'm Mum's age; it's looking
good.

10.30 a.m. Refill my bottle of water
from work's water cooler – notice that
Evian is just 'naïve' spelled backwards.
I can't be that dumb – this bottle has
lasted me a month.

Law 3:
Spend with
power

12.30 p.m. Josh calls to say the extra
loan on our mortgage has been
agreed. Yippee! That means we can
release enough from our house to pay
for the deposit on the holiday flat. We'll
rent it out most of the year but have
some free holidays, too. Am so excited;
all fits nicely with our long-term plan.

Law 5:
Look debt
in the face

Law 4:
Have goals

12.35 p.m. Remember Josh and I had
also discussed shopping around for car
insurance so I get some quotes online.
End up staying with the same insurer
but increasing the excess; that reduces
our premium by £60.

Law 3:
Spend with
power

12.45 p.m. Becky and I have lunch in our favourite café. One of my emotional triggers still pops up when the bill comes. Becky loves to pick up the tab, but we've opened up about money lately and I know she's been in debt. At my suggestion we split it. Tell her about the mortgage and the insurance. Dead impressed that she now puts her insurance on her credit card, pays it off at the end of the month and gets 5 per cent back. Must check out cash-back cards.

> Law 1:
> Take emotional control

> Law 6:
> Share financial intimacies

1.20 p.m. Walk back to work via the shoe shop. Last week I bought a gorgeous pair of Miu Miu heels to wear at a wedding on Saturday. Saw them in the sale yesterday reduced by £50 so bought another pair. I take back the original pair unworn (with receipt and bought less than twenty-eight days ago) and get refund! Funny, I used to be scared of returning things to shops. Now I know my rights and my consumer power. I leave the shop with a spring in my step and £50 better off. That can go towards the embroidered

> Law 3:
> Spend with power

> Law 1:
> Take emotional control

black jacket I've had my eye on,
perfect for business events and
evenings.

2.00 p.m. Meetings with new clients all
afternoon. Brian, my boss, praises me
for my handling of the European design
brief. Have finally shaken off my 'junior'
staff label. Arrange to meet and
discuss my salary with him. Know what
figure I'm after.

Law 2:
Go beyond
beliefs

5.30 p.m. Don't even notice the time
and am in a state of 'flow' as I finish off
the European job. Happy to work hard
if I'm doing what I love, I know if I work
for myself one day I'll have to put in
long hours.

Law 4:
Have goals

6.30 p.m. Josh is home before me and
has started making one of his delicious
vegetable curries. We have a relaxed
chat about the mortgage deal and new
car insurance figures. Then we do
some quick calculations together on
what our outgoings are going to be:
this type of thing used to terrify me but
now we do it regularly I'm fine with it.

Law 6:
Share financial
intimacies

Have a glass of Sancerre and congratulate Josh on his fantastic curry.

8.00 p.m. Do a few emails and check bank statement online. Feel more in control since I made this a weekly habit. Make note to self to research cash-back cards and business loans.

> Law 1:
> Take emotional control

9.00 p.m. Watch *Dragon's Den* on TV and am stunned at the lengths to which people will go to make their business idea work. A feisty, finger-on-the-pulse, no-nonsense female whose brainchild is an inspiring dot com business really wins over the dragons. Get a mental picture of me running a top-notch design service delivered online. Tell Josh of my five-year plan; very excited.

> Law 4:
> Have goals

11.00 p.m. Bedtime, feeling dead happy with how today has gone. Being a top Sheconomist, knowing I can enjoy life now and be in control of my future, means I can sleep peacefully again tonight.

> Being a top Sheconomist feels good!

THE SLIGHTLY CONFUSED GIRL'S GUIDE TO THE WORLD OF FINANCE

Additional State Pension (also known as State Second Pension or S2P) An additional pension, based on your earnings, which you may be entitled to on top of the *Basic State Pension* if you're an employee and not *Contracted out*. The S2P replaced the State Earnings Related Pension Scheme (or SERPs) in April 2002.

Additional Voluntary Contributions (AVCs) Top-up contributions you can make if you're in a company pension scheme. AVC schemes are run by your employer but you get to choose which funds to invest in.

Annual Equivalent Rate (AER) Rate of interest used to compare products that pay annual interest with ones that pay monthly on a like-for-like basis. If AERs are the same, the interest you'll receive will be identical whether it's paid monthly or annually.

Annuity A guaranteed income for life that an insurance company pays out in exchange for a pot of money from your pension plan.

Annual Percentage Rate (APR) Allows you to compare credit products by taking account of fees as well as the interest rate.

Assets Anything you own which has a monetary value, such as cash, savings, investments and property.

Bank base rate Interest rate set by the Bank of England and used by bank and building societies to set their saving and lending rates.

Bankruptcy A last resort legal procedure if you can't afford to repay your debts. It enables you to wipe the slate clean, although you would lose control of your assets (probably including your home). Declaring bankruptcy could also impact on your future life by closing down certain career routes and financial options.

Basic State Pension A pension paid by the government based on your National Insurance contributions. To receive the full amount, you need to have paid or been credited with sufficient *National Insurance* contributions.

Bonds A type of IOU agreement that allows companies or governments to borrow money from you at a fixed rate of interest over a specified period of time. *Government Bonds* are sometimes called Government Stock or Gilts. They usually pay less interest than *Corporate Bonds* (company IOUs) because they carry less risk.

Budget A statement which helps you plan how to allocate your expenses so that they don't exceed your income.

Buy-to-let A mortgage designed if you buy a property with the intention of renting it out.

Capital Money you have invested or saved.

Capital Gains Tax Tax due or paid on profits made from selling investments or other possessions.

Career Development Loan Helps you fund up to two years of learning. You don't have to start repaying the loan until a month after the course ends. No interest is charged while you're studying.

Cash Not only the notes and coins in your purse, but also money held in bank or building society accounts.
Cash ISA A way of saving up to £3,600 per tax year per person in a bank or building society account without having to pay tax on the interest.
Compound Interest Interest paid on the sum of your original investment or borrowing plus any interest that has accumulated.
Contracting Out A term which refers to contracting out of the *Additional State Pension.* When you contract out, the government pays part of your *National Insurance* contributions into a *Personal Pension* of your choosing. You decide how to invest the money and, at retirement, the fund provides you with income which replaces what you would have received from the *Additional State Pension* had you not contracted out.
Corporate Bonds See *Bonds*
Credit Rating or Credit Score Used by companies to assess your credit worthiness before agreeing to enter into a financial contract with you. A poor credit rating could jeopardize your chances of borrowing money at competitive rates or lead to rejected applications.
Credit Report A record of all your credit transactions, which gives potential *Creditors* an overview of how much credit you have available (such as limits on credit cards), whether you've missed any payments over the past six years or had any court action taken against you. It also shows whether you're on the electoral register.
Creditor Someone to whom you owe money.

Critical Illness Cover An insurance policy which pays out a lump sum if you contract a named critical condition such as cancer, stroke or heart attack.

Debt Management Plan A solution to paying off debt if you're unable to meet minimum payments. You agree with your creditors how you will pay back the debt based on what you can afford.

Discount brokers Companies that enable you to purchase financial products, such as investments or insurance, without giving you advice. These are sometimes known as 'execution-only' transactions. The company's charges or premiums are reduced on the basis that they don't provide advice.

Dividends Profits distributed by a company to its shareholders.

Endowment Policy An investment scheme designed to build up a lump sum at maturity (usually ten to twenty-five years) while paying out a guaranteed lump sum if you die before the policy matures.

Equities A holding in someone else's business, which could be in the form of *Shares* or *'Funds'*.

Equity (or Stocks and Shares) ISAs A way of investing up to £7,200 each tax year in *'Funds'* which grow tax efficiently.

Final Salary Company Pensions A type of pension offered by some employers. It provides you with a pension at retirement age based on your income when you stop working for them, and on the number of years you've been in the scheme.

Fixed Interest An agreed rate of interest over a specified period of type. *Bonds* are an example of a fixed interest product.

Free-standing Additional Voluntary Contributions (FSAVCs) Top-up contributions you can make if you're in a company pension scheme. FSAVC schemes are set up independently of your employer through an insurance or investment company of your choosing. It's also your choice which funds you invest in.

Friendly Society Bond A tax-free investment product that allows you to invest up to £25 a month.

FTSE (pronounced footsie) **100 Index** Represents the performance of the top 100 companies in the UK.

FTSE All Share Index Represents the performance of around the 700 largest companies in the UK.

'Fund' A term used to describe an investment into a collective package of *Shares* and/or *Bonds*. This allows you to combine your money with other investors, which spreads your investment risk across a range of different companies. Funds are usually managed by a *Fund Manager* who decides which companies to invest in and when to buy and sell the holdings. Unit trusts and Open Ended Investment Companies (OEICs) are both examples of '*Funds*'.

Fund Manager The person who is responsible for managing a '*Fund*'.

Government Bonds/Stock (Gilts) See *Bonds*

Group Personal Pensions A *Personal Pension* offered by your employer, which may have lower charges than a scheme that you arrange for yourself. Membership is not dependent on you continuing to be an employee.

Hire Purchase (HP) A way of buying goods, such as a car, where you pay a deposit followed by monthly repayments. You don't own the goods until you've made the final repayment.

Income Tax Tax that you pay on earned income as well as income received from *Savings, Pensions*, *Annuities* and taxable *Investments*.

Index Tracker See *Tracker Fund*

Individual Savings Account (ISA) A tax-efficient way of investing money either regularly or as a lump sum. You can invest in *Cash ISAs* or *Equity ISAs* and there are set limits that you can't exceed each tax year.

Individual Voluntary Arrangement (IVA) A formal proposal made by an insolvency practitioner to each organization you owe money to, asking them to wipe out part of your debt.

Inflation The rate at which the price of goods and service changes. The annual rate of inflation reflects the difference in price of a 'basket' of goods from one year to the next.

Inheritance Tax A tax that you may have to pay when you inherit money or assets from someone who has died.

Interest The amount that a lender charges for borrowing money, or that you earn when you're saving money.

Interest-only Mortgage Monthly payments which cover only the interest on the loan and not the money borrowed. At the end of the term you still owe the initial amount loaned and have to find a way of paying that off.

Investment Clubs A group of people who meet regularly to decide how to invest their collective pot of money. Members often invest just £25 a month. It's a fun way to learn about the stock market and dabble with making money.

Investments A way of building up money that's usually riskier and less accessible than *Savings* accounts. Unlike *Savings*, investments don't necessarily guarantee you'll get back what you put in. But they have greater potential for your money to grow.

Liabilities Anything you owe – such as *Mortgages*, *Loans*, credit cards, *HP* agreements or *Overdraft*.

Loans (secured) A loan where your lender has the right to the *Asset* secured against it, commonly your home, if you don't keep up the repayments.

Loans (unsecured) A loan which isn't secured against any of your *Assets.*

Money Purchase Company Pension A scheme where the amount of pension you receive depends on several factors: the amount paid in, how well it grows, the charges deducted and what income you can expect to receive from your *Annuity* (*Annuity* rate).

Mortgage A type of loan that you take out to purchase a property.

Mortgage Indemnity Premium (MIP) A one-off fee that a mortgage lender charges as insurance against any loss on selling the property if you default on the *Mortgage*. Some lenders insist on it if you are borrowing a high proportion of the value of the property, e.g. 90 per cent or more.

National Insurance (NI) A type of tax used to finance state benefits. For employees it gets deducted along with *Income tax* from your paycheque. If you're self-employed, you pay two types of NI – one is collected monthly and the other is paid when you pay your *Income tax*.

Net worth The difference between what you own (*Assets*) and what you owe (*Liabilities*).

Non-priority Debt Certain types of debt that carry less severe consequences than *Priority Debt* if you don't keep up the repayments. It includes: credit or store cards, *Overdrafts* and *Unsecured loans*.

Offset Mortgage A facility offered by some *Mortgage* lenders where you have the option of putting your savings in an account linked to your *Mortgage*. Rather than paying interest on the total amount you owe, you only pay interest on your *Mortgage* minus your savings.

Overdraft (authorized) A facility offered by your bank or building society which allows you to go into 'the red' on your current account. Many accounts offer a fee-free buffer but charge interest on any amount used above this.

Overdraft (unauthorized) This is where you go into 'the red' on your bank or building society account, without having first arranged this. You're likely to incur bank charges as a result and you'll pay interest on the amount you've effectively borrowed.

Pension A pot of money that you build up which you can't dip into before you reach a certain age, and there are restrictions about how much you can invest and how you draw the benefits once you have retired.

Personal Pension Available from insurance and investment companies. These work like a *Money Purchase Pension* and are especially suitable if you're self-employed or if your employer doesn't run a company scheme.

Permanent Health Insurance (PHI) A form of insurance that replaces part of your income if you can't work because of long-term illness or disability. The payout from this type of plan is usually restricted to a maximum proportion of your pre-illness pay (for example sixty per cent).

Power of Attorney A document that enables you to assign someone else legal responsibility for your financial affairs.

Priority debts Certain types of debt that carry more severe consequences than *Non-Priority Debt* if you don't keep up the repayments. It includes: *Mortgages*, rent, *Secured Loans*, council tax, utility bills, maintenance orders, some *Hire Purchase* agreements, *Income Tax*, *National Insurance*, VAT and court fines.

Private Medical Insurance (PMI) Insurance which pays your medical bills if you decide to 'go private'.

Protected Rights Part of a *Personal Pension* plan which builds up with money received from your *National Insurance* contributions as a result of *Contracting Out* of the *Additional State Pension*.

Remortgaging Replacing an existing *Mortgage* with another mortgage in an attempt to secure better terms or borrow more money. The new *Mortgage* pays off the old one.

Repayment Mortgage A type of *Mortgage* where your monthly payments gradually pay off the whole loan by the end of the agreed *Mortgage* term, as well as the interest.

Returns Any growth on an *Investment*.

Savings Placing your money with a bank or building society and earning interest in return.

Secured Loans See *Loans (secured)*.

Self Invested Personal Pensions (SIPPs) A *Personal Pension* plan where you get to make your own decisions about how to invest the contributions. It's like a DIY version of a *Pension*. You have more freedom and choice over how the '*Funds*' are invested.

Share Incentive Plan Plans provided by a company that offer you an incentive to buy shares in your employer's company.

Shares See *Equities*.

Sharesave or Save As You Earn (SAYE) Scheme A way of gradually saving towards buying *Shares* with your employer, pay tax efficiently and at a discount.

State Earnings Related Scheme (SERPS) *See Additional State Pension*

Share-based Investments *Investments* that are made through buying *Equities*.

Stakeholder Pensions Products that are similar to *Personal Pensions* but have low charges and can be more flexible than traditional schemes.

State Pension A pension paid by the government based on your *National Insurance* contributions. It's made up of two parts: the *Basic State Pension* and the *Additional State Pension*.

State Second Pension (S2P) See *Additional State Pension*.

Stock Market A market where you can buy and sell *Shares* and/or *Bonds*.

Stock Market Index A method of measuring the *Stock Market* over different time frames. The *FTSE 100 Index* and *FTSE All Share Index* are the most commonly used Indices in the UK to compare *Stock Market* performance.

Stocks and shares See *Equities*.

Student Loans Loans that are available from the government to help you pay for your studies. Nothing has to be paid back until you're in work and earning more than £15,000 a year. Interest is based on the rate of inflation.

Tracker Fund (sometimes known as an Index Tracker) A type of '*Fund*' that aims to replicate the performance of a chosen *Stock Market Index* such as the *FTSE All Share Index* by investing in the same companies as those included in that index. The charges are often cheaper than a '*Fund*' actively managed by a *Fund Manager*.

Unsecured loans See *Loans (unsecured)*.

Volatility A term often used when talking about *Share-based Investments*. It measures how much the value of a *Share* or '*Fund*' deviates from its average over a period of time. The higher the volatility, the greater the risk.

Index

Note: Page numbers in *italic* denote entries
in the glossary section.

addictive tendencies (shopping)
  80–84
Additional State Pension 303, *327*
Additional Voluntary Contributions
  (AVC) schemes 304, *327*
advertising 65–8
advice agencies (debt) 204–05, 255
AER (Annual Equivalent Rate) 286,
  327
alternatives to shopping 71–2, 79,
  106–13
anger-driven spending 19–20,
  40–41, 75
Annual Equivalent Rate (AER) 286,
  327
Annual Percentage Rate (APR)
  286, *327*
annuities 301, *327*
antiques 295–296
APR (Annual Percentage Rate)
  286, *327*
art 295–96
assets *327*
AVC (Additional Voluntary
  Contributions) schemes 304,
  327
aversion to money 20–21

bank base rate 298, *327*
bankruptcy 211–12, *328*
bargaining 23, 100, 194, 195–6
bargains 27–8, 74
beliefs about money **32–62**
  case studies 35–6, 38–9,
    40–42, 43–5, 56–8
  changing 34–7, 53–61
  checklist 62
  earnings levels 47–50
  millionaires 51–2
  recognizing 37–42, 52–3
  self-efficacy 45–7
  self-fulfilling 37
  unrealistic 42–5
best deals, locating 98–100, 101,
  214
bills, paying 98–9, 217–18
bonds 139, 290, 292–4, *328*
borrowing *see* debt
budgets *see* spending plans
business start-up loans 164
Buy Nothing Days 72
buy-to-let mortgages 166, *328*

capital *328*
capital gains tax 248, 249, *328*

career-related debt 163–4, *328*
cash 79, 103, 278, *329*
cash flow 90–96, 98, 115–17, 231
cash ISAs 139, 265, 285, *329*
cash withdrawals (credit cards) 180
cash-back deals 167, 209
charges *see* fees and charges
childhood, origins of money attitudes and beliefs 24–9, 234–35
children 240–46
Citizens Advice Bureau 204
clothes 67–71
clubs, investment 294–5, *333*
co-dependent spending 74–5
compensatory consumption 81
competitive spending 73
compound interest 176–8, *329*
consolidating debts 181–2, 198–200
consumer confidence 72–3
Consumer Credit Counselling Service 204
contracting out (Additional State Pension) *329*
contributions (pensions) 304, 306–07
cooking 110
credit cards 104, 165–7, 173–4
    see also debt; store cards
    cash withdrawals 180
    cash-back deals 167
    destroying 195–6, 199
    funding day-to-day living 180–81
    interest 181, 198–9, 286
    interest-free deals 98, 166–7, 172–3

repayments 178, 179, 189–91, 196–7, 202
credit levels (UK) 162–3
credit rating/score 170–72, 197, *329*
credit reports 170–71, 197, *329*
creditors 203–4, *329*
critical illness cover *330*
current accounts 209

dates (relationships) 217–18
day in the life of a top Sheconomist 321–26
day-to-day living, funded by credit cards 180
death of partner 249, 251, 252
    see also inheritances
debt **160–214**
    see also credit cards
    advice agencies 204–06, 256
    assets that are liabilities 173
    blogs 256
    borrowing to invest 168–70
    career-related 167–8, *328*
    case studies 160–61, 189–95, 205–08
    checklist 213
    consolidation 181–2, 198–200
    consumer credit levels 162–3
    credit rating 170–72, 197, *329*
    and emotional crises 182–3
    emotional responses to 191–2
    funding other debt 175, 181
    hire purchase 198, *332*
    listing 185–6
    loans secured against home 181
    management plans 185–8, 193–5, 196, 204–07, 214, *330*
    negotiating with creditors 203–04

overdrafts 172–3, 181, 286,
  334
perspectives on 163–4
protection plans 199, 300
psychologically harmful 176
store cards 179, 180, 181, 197
unmanageable 210–12
Debt-Free Me visualization 200
delayed gratification 84–7, 183
devaluation of assets 173
direct debits 103
discount brokers *330*
discounted mortgages 298
disgust 20–22
dividends 292, 317, *330*

earnings levels 47–50
emotional response to money
  8–31
  case study 25
  checklist 31
  debt 182–3, 186–7
  money personalities 29–30
  negative emotions 13–24
  origins in childhood 24–9,
    234–5
  reconditioning 30
  Ultimatum Game 12
endowment policies 299, *330*
equities (stocks and shares)
    139–40, 278, 279–80,
    289–92, *330*
  see also investments
  dividends 292, 317, *330*
  funds (general) 289, 291–2, *331*
  investment clubs 294–5, *333*
  ISAs 139, 289, 292, 316–17, *330*
  share schemes 275–6, *336*
  sweepstakes 288

extra money, making 39–40,
    208–10
extras (film and television) 213

fashion industry 68–9
fear 15–19
fees and charges (financial
    products) 200, 210, 289, 300
Final Salary company pensions
    304, *330*
financial coaches/therapists 256
Financial Services Authority (FSA)
    22
fixed interest 278, 298, *331*
food 101–02, 111
Free-Standing Additional Voluntary
    Contributions (FSAVCs) *331*
friendly society bonds 290, *331*
friends
  buying property with 299
  investment clubs 294–5, *333*
  money envy 222–5
  presents 74–5, 224–5, 224
  share sweepstakes 288
  sharing financial intimacies 201,
    216–7, 233, 259
  shopping with 18, 79
FSA (Financial Services Authority)
    22
FSAVCs (Free-Standing Additional
    Voluntary Contributions) *331*
FTSE indices 291, *331*
fuel bills 98–9
fund managers *331*
funds 289, 291–2, *331*
  see also Individual Savings
    Accounts
future, securing **261–320**
  for major subjects *see* goals;

investments; pensions;
    savings
case study 267–9
checklist 320
employer benefits 275–6
false sense of security 273–5
financial ignorance/literacy 265,
    277–9
gender-specific factors 313–14
ignoring 269–75, 312–13
insurance 317–19
letter to future self 320
planning with partner 246–52
risk 279–81

gardening 111
giving away money 22, 109–10
goals **121–59**
    see also future, securing;
        savings; spending plans
    age-specific 130–34
    benefits of 125–7
    case studies 127–9, 153–7
    checklist 159
    financial amounts, calculating
        134
    maintaining 147–8
    making extra money 39–40
    net worth 140–46
    setting 136–40, 150–53, 158
        long-term 138, 140, 141,
            152
        medium-term 138, 139, 141,
            152
        short-term 138–9, 141,
            151–2
    small steps 149, 151–3
    top five Sheconomist goals 135
    visualization 113, 129

Group Personal Pension schemes
    305, *332*
gyms 100

habitual spending 73–80
Hardy, Catherine 212–13
health insurance 135, 317, *330*,
    335
hiding spending and financial
    affairs from partner 252–8
hire purchase (HP) 198, *332*
holidays 220–2
home ownership *see* property
home, working from 208
HP (hire purchase) 198, *332*

ignorance (money matters) 22,
    45–7, 282–4
income tax *see* tax
Individual Savings Accounts (ISAs)
    332
    see also funds; savings
        accounts
    cash 139, 265, 285, *329*
    equity 139, 289, 292, 316–17,
        330
Individual Voluntary Arrangements
    (IVAs) 210–11, *332*
inflation *332*
inheritances 249–50, 284–5, *332*
    see also death of partner
insurance policies 99–100, 317–19
    health 135, 317, *330*, *335*
    life 135, 317, 318, 319
    mortgages 300, *333–4*
    travel 221–2
interest *332*
    AER/APR 286, *327*
    best deals 172–3, 203, 209

borrowing to invest 168–70
compound 176–8, *334*
credit cards 172, 198–9, 286
current accounts 209
fixed 278, 298, *331*
mortgages 174–5, 181, 197,
201–2, 286, 298–9, *333*
savings accounts 281, 284,
285, 286
interest-free deals (credit cards)
98, 166–7, 172–3
interest-only mortgages 173–4,
197, 201–02, 298–9, *333*
internet 23–4, 261
investment clubs 294–5, *333*
investments 278, **286–301**, *333*
for major subjects *see* equities;
property; savings
alternative 295–6
borrowing to invest 168–70
case study 292–4
choosing 287–8
couples 248
goals 138–40
returns 292–4, 296, *336*
tax-efficient 288, 289, 290, 302
top tips 289–90
ISAs *see* Individual Savings
Accounts
IVAs (Individual Voluntary
Arrangements) 210–11, *332*

joint accounts 226–31

letters, to future self 320
liabilities 173, *331*
life insurance 135, 317, 318, 319
logs 57–9, 90
lost money, finding 209, 311–12

lying to partner about spending
and financial affairs 252–8

market research 209
mean men 240
millionaires 51–2
mind-expanding activities 112
mindsets, money 60–61, 232–6
MIP (Mortgage Indemnity
Premium) 300, *333–4*
money envy 222–5
money personalities 29–30
Money Purchase company
pensions 304, *333*
Mortgage Indemnity Premium
(MIP) 301, *333–4*
mortgages 297–301, *333*
see also property
as bad debt 174–5
buy-to-let 170, *328*
case study 207
comparing 299
duration 301
fees and charges 300
goals 135
as good debt 164–5, 169–70
insurance 300, *333–4*
interest 172, 174–5, 181, 202,
206–7, 291, 303–4, *338*
remortgaging 169–70, 175,
206, *335–6*
repayment options 201–02,
298–99
savings-linked 285
switching lenders 301

narcissistic spending 74
National Debtline, The 205
national insurance 186, *334*

nature, enjoyment of 113
net worth 140–46, 265–6, *334*
non-priority debt 203–4, *334*

occasional expenses 104, 135
offset accounts 285, *334*
organizing finances 17
overdrafts 172–3, 181, 286, *334*

partners *see* spouses and partners
pay levels 47–50
payment protection insurance
    (PPI) 198, 300
Payplan 205
pensions 252, 261–5, **301–17**,
    335
    alternatives to 316–17
    case studies 307–08, 311,
        315
    company pensions, desirability
        265, 275
    contributions 304, 306–08
    failure to join schemes 312–13
    lost policies 311–12
    options (schemes) 304–06
    projected income 306–10
    reviewing 310
    state pension 261–2, 303, 315,
        327, *328*, *337*
    tax-relief 302, 307–08
Permanent Health Insurance (PHI)
    335
Personal Pension schemes 305,
    335
petrol prices 99
PHI (Permanent Health Insurance)
    335
PMI (Private Medical Insurance)
    335

pocket money (children) 244, 245
power of attorney 319, *335*
PPI (payment protection
    insurance) 198, 300
presents 74–5, 218–20, 224
priority debt 185–6, 203–04, 214,
    335
private letting relief 249
Private Medical Insurance (PMI)
    335
property 278, 296–301
    see also investments;
        mortgages
    buying with friends 299
    costs of buying 300
    couples 249–50
    investment potential 296–7
    loans secured against home 181
protected rights *335*
protection plans (repayments) 203,
    300
publications (investment products)
    289
purses 87–9

RAM (Running Away Money) 229
records (spending) 89–96, 98,
    104, 115–17, 231
reference anxiety 18–19
relationships *see* spouses and
    partners
remortgaging 169–70, 175, 201,
    335–6
repayment mortgages 201–02,
    298, *336*
retirement *see* future, securing
retraining 167
revenge spending *see*
    anger-driven spending

risk 279–81
Rule of 72 (investment returns) 296
Running Away Money (RAM) 229

S2P (State Second Pension) *327*
save-as-you-earn (SAYE) schemes 275, *336*
savings *336*
  see also future, securing; goals; investments
  case studies 282–3, 311
  compound interest 176–8, *329*
  delaying 131–2
savings accounts 139, 281–6
  see also Individual Savings Accounts
  interest 281, 284, 285, 286
  mortgage-linked 285
savings schemes (employers) 275, 276
SAYE (save-as-you-earn) schemes 275, *336*
secured loans 181, *333*
Self Invested Personal Pensions (SIPPs) 305, *336*
self-efficacy in money matters 45–7, 265
selling (eBay) 214
SERPS (State Earnings Related Pension Scheme) *336*
7 Laws of Sheconomics 7
shame 22–4
share incentive plans *336*
shares *see* equities
sharesave schemes 280, *336*
sharing financial intimacies *see* friends; spouses and partners

shopping *see* spending
SIPPs (Self Invested Personal Pensions) 305, *336*
spending, compulsive
  addictive tendencies 80–84
  anger-driven 19–20, 40–41, 75
  combating *see* spending with power
  fear-driven 18
  hiding from partner 252–8
  shame 23–4
  spending habits 73–80
spending plans **96–106**, *328*
  see also goals
  best deals, locating 98–100, 101
  example 118–20
  food shopping 101–02
  maintaining 103–05
  monitoring 102–03
  rules 100
spending with power **63–120**
  addictive tendencies 80–84
  alternatives to shopping 71–2, 79, 106–13
  case study 77–8, 93–4
  checklist 114
  consumer confidence 72–3
  delayed gratification 84–7
  habitual spending 73–80
  purses (indicators) 87–9
  resisting pressure/temptation 65–72
  spending plans *see* spending plans (above)
  tracking spending 89–96, 98, 104, 115–17, 236
  visualization 113

spouses and partners, death of 249, 251, 252
spouses and partners, sharing financial intimacies **215–60**
  admitting financial problems 255–9
  case studies 247, 256–8
  checklist 260
  children 240–46
  communication 236–7
  early stages of relationship 217–18
  hiding spending and financial affairs from 252–8
  holidays 220–22
  joint accounts 226–31
  money mindsets 232–6
  planning financial future 246–52
  presents 218–19
  properties 249–50
  source of conflict 225–6
  tax considerations 248–50
Stakeholder Pension schemes 305, *336*
standard variable rate mortgages 298
State Earnings Related Pension Scheme (SERPS) *336*
state pension 261–2, 303, 315, *327*, *328*, *337*
State Second Pension (S2P) *327*
statements, financial 253–4
stock market *337*
stocks *see* equities

store cards 179, 180, 181, 197
  see also credit cards
student loans 167–8, *337*
sweepstakes (shares) 288

targets *see* goals
tax 248–50, *332*
  capital gains 248, 249, *328*
  credits 208
  inheritance 249–50, *332*
  on interest 284, 285
  relief (pensions) 302, 307–08
tax-efficient investments 288, 289, 290, 302
telephone tariffs 99
text messages 222
thrift, enjoying 111–12
tracker funds 291, *337*
tracker-rate mortgages 298
transfer fees (credit cards) 172
travel insurance 219–22
treats, small 79

Ultimatum Game 12
unmanageable debt 210–12
unsecured loans 181, 200, *333*
utility bills 98–9

visualization 113, 129, 200
volatility *337*

wage levels 47–50
wills 319
wine 295–6